Miriam's Farm

The Story of Haggs Farm,
the Chambers family
and D.H. Lawrence

Edited by Clive Leivers

Five Leaves Publications
in association with
The Haggs Farm Preservation Society

Miriam's Farm
The Story of Haggs Farm,
the Chambers family
and D.H. Lawrence

Published by Five Leaves
in association with
The Haggs Farm Preservation Society

Miriam's Farm was first published in 2017
by The Haggs Farm Preservation Society

ISBN: 9781915434074

Collection copyright:
Haggs Farm Preservation Society

www.fiveleaves.co.uk
www.fiveleavesbookshop.co.uk
www.haggsfarmsociety.co.uk

Typeset by 4 Sheets Design and Print

Printed in Great Britain

... some of my happiest days I've spent haymaking in the fields just opposite the south side of Greasley church ... Miriam's father hired those fields ... Walk up Engine Lane, over the level crossing to Moorgreen pit, along till you come to the highway ... you come to the lodge gate by the reservoir ... (go) on through the wood to Felley Mill and go up the footpath to Annesley ... That's the country of my heart. From the hills, if you look across at Underwood Wood, you'll see a tiny red farm on the edge of the wood. That was Miriam's farm — where I got my first incentive to write.

D.H. Lawrence to Rolf Gardiner 3 December 1926

Haggs Farm Preservation Society

The Society was formed in 1986 to encourage the preservation of the farm buildings and to reinforce the vital importance of the farm to the formative years of D.H. Lawrence's development as a writer.

The aims of the Society are:-

To promote interest in and as opportunity arises, to be actively involved with the preservation of the buildings, with the aim of securing some form of public access.

To research and publicise the history of the farm, its tenants and the Lawrence connection

To find out more please visit
the Haggs Farm Preservation Society website.

www.haggsfarmsociety.co.uk

Dedication

This book is dedicated to the memory of Professor Jonathan David Chambers and Ann Howard. David Chambers, the youngest of the Chambers children, was born at Haggs Farm in 1898 and was mainly responsible for securing listed building status for the farm. Ann Howard, his daughter, played a leading role in the formation of the Haggs Farm Preservation Society, remaining a constant supporter throughout her life.

Clive Leivers, 1938–2022
Clive Leivers became Chairman of the Haggs Farm Preservation Society soon after its foundation in 1986. His affinity to the Haggs went back to his childhood, he was born and brought up in Underwood and his grandad was born at Haggs Farm. Clive credited his upbringing in the rural environment of Underwood for his love of the countryside, love of music and love of literature. As chair of the society, Clive worked tirelessly to raise awareness of Haggs Farm and remind people of its literary significance, never wavering in his aim of ensuring its conservation and maybe one day its restoration. He edited two books, *Miriam's Farm* and *Lawrence's Muse: Jessie Chambers Wood through her own writing*, both essential reading for anyone wanting to find out more about the history of the Haggs, D.H. Lawrence and Jessie Chambers. Clive Leivers died in 2022 while *Lawrence's Muse* was in press.

The Haggs Farm from above Felley Mill

Contents

Acknowledgements

The use of Jessie Chambers' letters in Chapter 10 is by permission of Inspire Nottinghamshire Archives. The story by May Holbrook (Chapter 5) is published by permission of Nottingham University Manuscripts and Special Collections and Mrs Ann Howard. The transcript of David Chambers' interview with Tony Church (Chapter 8) and the photograph on the dedication page are used by courtesy of Nottingham Local Studies Library, Angel Row, Nottingham.

All other photographs are from the collections of Mrs Ann Howard and the Society.

Preface

"You Haggites see the best in me"

D.H. Lawrence and the Haggs

John Worthen

According to Jessie Chambers, D.H. Lawrence said more than once — 'ah, you Haggites see the best of me!'[1] He said it (according to Jessie) 'whimsically' but it leaves us not only with the question 'why was that?' but with the more worrying query: 'what was he like when you didn't see the best of him?'

We should look again at the famous letter Lawrence wrote on 15 November 1928 about the Haggs: mailed from the island of Port-Cros in the Mediterranean.

Dear David

I hardly recognized you as J.D. — and you must be a man now, instead of a thin little lad with very fair hair. Ugh, what a gap in time! it makes me feel scared.

Whatever I forget, I shall never forget the Haggs — I loved it so. I loved to come to you all, it really was a new life began in me there. The waterpippin by the door — those maiden-blush roses that Flower (the horse) would lean over and eat — and Trip (the bull-terrier) floundering round — And stewed figs for tea in winter, and in August green stewed apples. Do you still have them? Tell your mother I never forget, no matter where life carries us. — And does she still blush if somebody comes and finds her in a dirty white apron? or doesn't she wear work-aprons any more? Oh I'd love to be nineteen again, and coming up through the Warren and catching the first glimpse of the buildings. Then I'd sit on the sofa under the window, and we'd crowd round the little table to tea, in that tiny little kitchen I was so at home in.

Son' tempi passati, cari miei! quanto cari, non saprete mai! — I could never tell you in English how much it all meant to me, how I still feel about it.

If there is anything I can ever do for you, do tell me. — Because whatever else I am, I am somewhere still the same Bert who rushed with such joy to the Haggs.

Ever

D.H. Lawrence[2]

7

We all get involved in the myths of our own lives; we start to enact the feelings which we tell ourselves we should have had. But however lovely the letter, we will probably be most struck by its devouring nostalgia, of a kind in which Lawrence very rarely engaged (it's hard to think of another example, not even in his writing about the Kiowa ranch, a place he regretted long and deeply). The letter is also remarkable for what it misses out — for example, actually telling David Chambers how much the Haggs means to him. Lawrence puts it in Italian and not many of the Chambers family, if any, would have understood it. And he adds that he couldn't say it in English (it means 'there are times past, my dears! how dear, you will never know!'). No, the Chambers family would indeed never know, Lawrence deliberately hides it.

The other striking thing is that Lawrence's account of being nineteen (in 1904) means that he is able to leave out any mention of Jessie Chambers and those years of strain between 1906 and 1912, with their eventual emotional and sexual disaster. This was perhaps tactful; he must have known that how he had treated Jessie might still be a sore subject in the Chambers family, who would — for a while at least — have believed that he had left her most horribly in the lurch. And in turn David Chambers was very careful neither to tell Jessie he had been in touch with Lawrence, nor to tell her what was in the reply (or not said). But in Lawrence's recreation of the Haggs in this extraordinary glow of memory, it was on the still living memory of the place and the family, the warmth of the home, back in 1904, which he concentrated. He was not thinking of the loss of any of them. From 1902 to 1904, what mattered was discovering how happily he could be 'at home' at the Haggs: and he gave to the Chambers family as richly and lovingly as they gave to him. Sarah Ann Chambers loved him 'like one of her own' and he loved her; he was devoted to Alan; and with the family he could be the lively and cheerful son he found it impossible to be in Eastwood. Above all else, the Haggs offered unconditional love and companionship: things for which he went on looking during the rest of his life.

The Port-Cros letter was written in the late autumn of 1928, after the publication of *Lady Chatterley's Lover* earlier in the year. The Lawrences had left the Villa Mirenda near Florence in June 1928 and spent July and August at altitude in Switzerland, hoping to harden up Lawrence's lungs: a task made harder by the fact that they had decided together that he was not suffering from TB, only from chronic bronchitis. He had actually had a wretched summer, unable to walk far because the place they'd rented, Gsteig bei Gstaad, was — at 4,000 feet — on the edge of an Alp, incredibly steep in all directions. Once up there, in the chalet Kesselmatte, Lawrence was in effect marooned: and they had taken it for a couple of months. Finally, they came down, to see Frieda's mother in Baden-Baden; and while there the Lawrences finally decided to give up the Villa Mirenda, their current home. Although they had enjoyed living there, the Mirenda was now irresistibly linked in Lawrence's mind with his haemorrhages of July 1927. Places he associated with illness (like Oaxaca and Mexico City) he never wanted to go back to, and he was now convinced that the Mirenda 'didn't suit my health'. Frieda returned to the Mirenda to see to the packing up of their belongings; Lawrence waited for her alone in the Mediterranean port of Le Lavandou, near Toulon. They had been invited for the winter to the island of Port-Cros, where Richard Aldington, Arabella Yorke and Brigit Patmore (whom they had known for years) had taken a house. This must have appealed to Lawrence, after the failure of altitude to do him any good: Mediterranean air would surely be better.

Aldington was, however, malicious when he commented that Frieda's task of giving up the Mirenda was: 'a complicated process, since it involved a journey to Trieste'.[3] Frieda had started her affair with Angelo Ravagli. Lawrence could do nothing except sit and wait; he did not yet know what was happening, though he certainly suspected.

The Vigie was a borrowed house at the top of the island of Port-Cros: another place with the most marvellous view. Although Lawrence liked the place, and the island, and liked the people there, he was far too short of breath to take part in their expeditions. The steepness of the road up to the Vigie meant that he was 'perched, as at Kesselmatte', and could not for example accompany the others when they went swimming. Frieda, too, had come back from Italy (and Ravagli) with a cold, which of course Lawrence instantly caught. He had 'two days hemorrhage' and felt 'rather rotten'.[4] When Brigit took his breakfast to him in bed in the morning, and put a coat round his shoulders, 'I could feel his pyjamas soaked with perspiration.'

It was while they were on the island, too, that Lawrence got a letter which included some of the responses to *Lady Chatterley* appearing in the English press: *John Bull*'s notorious review, and a piece in the *Sunday Chronicle*. The group read them aloud, with shouts of hilarity: this is Brigit Patmore's account.

> 'My God!' one of us gave a shout. 'Here, in this one, Lorenzo, one of them calls you a cesspool!'

He made a grimace which might have been a smile or slight nausea.

> 'Really? One's fellow creatures are too generous. It's quite worth while giving of one's best, isn't it?' Then, as if speaking to himself, 'Nobody *likes* being called a cesspool'.[5]

In fact, we know the press cutting had not said that Lawrence was a cesspool, but that his novel was. The person must have shouted out 'One of them calls *Lady C* a cesspool!' And Lawrence must have responded 'Nobody *likes* their novel being called a cesspool'.

But various things went wrong at La Vigie, apart from those reviews. For one thing, Lawrence accidentally discovered that Frieda was indeed having an affair with Ravagli. For another, Aldington was starting an affair with Brigit Patmore, and both the Lawrences sided with Arabella Yorke, of whom they were very fond. Lawrence ended up violently angry with Aldington. His poem 'I know a noble Englishman,' probably begun at La Vigie, would assert that 'Ronald never wants a woman, he doesn't like women' because 'he's an instinctive homosexual'[6] Aldington never forgave Lawrence for that.

And Lawrence was thoroughly depressed and miserable. One afternoon while the others were off swimming — they bathed, Aldington recalled with relish more than thirty years later, *'naked* daily together on one of the plages of Port-Cros, and then lay in the sun' — Lawrence told Brigit Patmore how he had always found that 'you have something in your life which makes up for everything, and then find you haven't got it'. He might have meant Frieda: *but* she never had been loyal. He meant sexual desire. And whether they meant to or not, Frieda, Brigit and Aldington (and in her own way poor Arabella) were making horribly clear to him the continuing importance of sexual desire in their own lives. Brigit tried to tell him that his writing had mattered immensely to her in re-establishing her own sense of herself after she had been ill; but found she was only making matters worse. Lawrence replied: 'Yes. Once I could do that. I can't any more'[7] In the past, he could convey his intimate experience of the body and its desires directly in his writing. That was gone too; such writing was now either nostalgic or reminiscent.

And it was at this point that the letter from Jessie Chambers' younger brother David came, and he wrote that famous response. Its nostalgia — for a time when he was well, young, desiring, surrounded by others — is palpable. Its almost desperate reminiscence of the old days — 'whatever else I am, I am somewhere still the same Bert who rushed with such joy to the Haggs'[8] — is that of a man who has left all that terribly far behind him, and who indeed wondered whether he still *was* the same Bert. It's an odd formulation: 'Whatever else I am' — as if he feared that he *had* indeed changed, into something he didn't like very much (a lonely, non-desiring, sick man). He actually uses the formulation twice in the letter: 'whatever else I am' and 'Whatever I forget' suggesting that there was indeed much else that he might forget, in his own life (his own later relationship with Jessie, for one thing: a silent presence in the letter).

The warmth of the Chambers family and the time glowed all the more vividly not only because of the weakened physical state in which he now existed, but because it was tantalising as an idea of what a group of people, happily together, might be like: and it made him despair. Away from the Haggs he had never had that familial warmth, that love: and had always insisted he did not want it. But now, on Port-Cros, living the life of an invalid, cut off from the lively everyday concerns of the people he was with, with those reviews of *Lady Chatterley* reminding him how much he was hated in England, he must have felt more alone than ever. And he was more cut off from Frieda than he had been since 1912. Well, he had always wanted to be independent. But oh to be nineteen again ...

His response to David Chambers, therefore, tells us far more about Lawrence in 1928 than it does about the Lawrence of 1904. Both the joy and the despair underlying it belong to that very difficult complex of feelings around home, and belonging, and being part of a group, and being alone, which had existed in him since he was a teenager.

So what had he meant, so many years earlier, when he had said to the Chambers family, 'Ah, you Haggites see the best of me'? What was it that he was all too aware of, but which they didn't see?

The answer must be the culture of his own family, his own peculiar variety of Eastwood. For his letter makes him sound exactly like Arthur Lawrence escaping Lydia Lawrence, doing his best to leave behind the strictness of home and its moral absolutes, the things which usually governed him, for warmth and people and uncritical companionship. It was at the Haggs that Lawrence seemed most like Arthur: May Chambers' fiancé Will Holbrook recalled how Lawrence 'loved to come where he could do and say just what he pleased, even to using strong language to win his point'.[9] He sang with the Chambers family (his father had been in the choir of St James's Church at Brinsley as a boy), and demonstrated how he could dance 'in our little kitchen, and once while we paused for breath he said: father says one ought to be able to dance on a threepenny bit'.[10] Jessie, knowing Lawrence's hatred of his father, was surprised at that little revelation; but Lawrence also demonstrated his talent (his father's too) for mimicry. One set piece was a long-drawn-out row between his father and his mother which took Arthur's side and reduced its listeners to helpless laughter: 'even mother had to laugh'.[11] David Chambers, again, remembered: 'I think everyone loved him at this time; he combined with his vivacity a sweetness of disposition that was quite irresistible'.[12] That was the 'best of me' which the Haggites saw, even if it were only part of him — and certainly not the dutiful, detached and analytical part. The Chambers family never forgot him: when he died in 1930, 'We all, as a family, mourn him, for the memories of old days were unspeakably dear to us all'.[13]

And in 1928 it had been so sweet to recall the Haggs, to relive it, to vanish into it for a moment: the lost self of nineteen years old, for a moment recovered. In a life so full of radical change, it was vitally important to Lawrence that, somehow, neither he nor the Haggs should change: 'whatever else I am, I am somewhere still the same Bert who rushed with such joy to the Haggs'. Somewhere ...

Notes

1   J.D. Chambers, 'Memories of D.H. Lawrence' *Renaissance and Modern Studies*, xvi (1972), 12; T. 134.
2   *Letters*, vi. 618.
3   Nehls, iii. 253
4   *Letters*, vi. 593; Nehls, iii.253; *Letters*, vi.598.
5   Nehls, iii. 260.
6   '(I Know a Noble Englishman)', *The Complete Poems of D.H. Lawrence*, ed. Vivian de

Sola Pinto and Warren Roberts (London, 1967), i. 953–55.

7   Richard Addlington to H.D., 17October 1960 (*Richard Addlington & H.D.*, ed. C. Zilboorg, p251); Nehls III. 258.

8   *Letters*, vi. 618.

9   *Letters*, i. Nehls, iii. 611.

10 ET. 30.

11 ET. 32.

12 J.D. Chambers, 'Memories' p.12 E.T. 134.

13 *Collected Letters* 49.

Chapter 1
The history of the farm and its tenants
Clive Leivers

Introduction

In his letter to Rolf Gardiner, Lawrence described the countryside which was 'the country of my heart'; he referred specifically to Miriam's Farm.

Miriam Leivers was the heroine of Lawrence's novel *Sons and Lovers*. The character is closely based on that of Jessie Chambers, whose family were the tenants of Haggs Farm near Underwood in Nottinghamshire in the first decade of the twentieth century. The farm is now uninhabited and derelict but is a Grade II listed building because of the Lawrence connection. The other cottage on the site, New Haggs, is also a listed building and this account will include some mention of its history and tenants.

Haggs Farm lies about three miles from the mining town of Eastwood where Lawrence was born and at the north western corner of the parish of

Greasley; the nearest settlement is the village of Underwood, about a mile away along the farm track and Felley Mill Lane. The name of Greasley Haggs, the area in which the farm lies, obviously relates to a clearing within the western fringes of Sherwood forest.

This narrative draws on the extensive records of the Melbourne estate[1] which owned the farm until 1916 and the descriptions of the buildings found in the writings of Lawrence and members of the Chambers family. On the sale of the Melbourne property in Nottinghamshire in 1916, the farm and much of the surrounding countryside was bought by the Barber family, the colliery owners living at nearby Lamb Close. The records relating to Barber ownership are not open to public scrutiny and therefore the history of the farm in the last 50 years or so of its occupation is based upon restricted evidence.

The first mention of Haggs Farm as such is found in an estate valuation of 1805 which records two tenants:

> In the possession of John Leivers, tenant at will, at a yearly rent of £8 10s 3d. A cottage with a small barn and cowhouse built at the tenants expense. Brick walls, part tiled, part thatched. Part of Hagg closes taken from A Jackson's Farm.
>
> In the possession of James Anthony, tenant at will, at a yearly rent of £7 17s 6d. A cottage in middling repair, a small barn and cowhouse. Brick and tiled, built at the tenants expense.
>
> 10 acres, part of Hagg closes, taken from Mr Jackson's Farm.

There is no mention of the buildings or the tenants in a survey taken 10 years earlier, and it therefore seems most probable that the cottages were built sometime between 1795 and 1805. The Leivers and Anthony families were to continue as tenants for most of the nineteenth century, but before attempting to depict their lives at the Haggs, we can trace some of the earlier history of the area.

Greasley Haggs in the Seventeenth and Eighteenth Centuries

The area known as Greasley Haggs was part of the lands held by the Carthusian priory of Beauvale, a mile or so away, and was perhaps part of the 300 acres in Greasley mentioned in the original grant of lands by Nicholas de Cantilupe in 1343. When, on the dissolution of the monasteries, Sir William Hussey was granted the Beauvale lands, a Patent Roll of 1550 contains some familiar local names and a specific mention of the Haggs:-

> ... the parcell called Callys Hagge and Hye Parke, the woods called Wylley ... the wood, enclosure and close in Wylley called Conygre ... the pasture and close called Hagge Lease in tenure of Robert Levys (and) ... the close and pasture called Lambe Close.

The Beauvale lands granted to Hussey soon came into the hands of the Morison family and from thence to the Capells who became the Earls of Essex.

The estate was eventually purchased in 1752 by Matthew Lamb, whose descendants were to be ennobled as the Lords Melbourne with their seat at Melbourne Hall in Derbyshire. By 1879 the family held over 5,000 acres of land in Nottinghamshire, a good part of which was in the parishes of Greasley and Selston. The Nottinghamshire estate was eventually dismembered in 1916. The records of the Melbourne estate, though fragmentary for the early part of the period, do enable us to trace the history of the area from the seventeenth century onwards with some degree of certainty. Some supporting information is also contained in surviving wills of the tenants.

On 20 November 1626 Francis Cocke, a yeoman of Underwood, made his will. He referred to land held of Sir Charles Morison including Great Willey and South Willey in the parish of Greasley and two closes called the Hagges.[2] In 1653 a survey of her Beauvale estate was conducted for Dame Elizabeth Capell. This included three references to the area of Greasley Haggs covering some 101 acres. Firstly John Burton was renting a house and grounds called the Haggs, totalling just over 35 acres at an annual rent of £12/6/8. The second tenant was Francis Cocke (the son of the testator of 1626) who rented 49 acres at a rent of £16/7/0. Lastly there was Charles Sheppard who had just over 17 acres at a rent of £7/2/0.

And it is the land rented by Sheppard that provides the link to the first trace of Haggs Farm. Charles Sheppard was the tenant of Bagthorpe Manor Farm and by 1675 had been succeeded by his son Richard, who himself died in 1678. In 1717 Richard's grandson, Richard Wood, was the tenant of Manor Farm and was still renting the 17 acres comprising the three closes called the Haggs. By 1747 Wood had been succeeded as tenant at Bagthorpe by Richard Jackson. In addition to renting 76 acres at Bagthorpe, Jackson was also the tenant of 190 acres in and around Moorgreen with his homestead at Shortwood. The tenancy included the three Haggs Closes which were formerly part of Hall Farm at Bagthorpe. It was from the Jackson Farm, according to the 1805 survey, that John Leivers and James Anthony had been given their smallholdings of around ten acres apiece.

The first Tenants: Leivers and Anthony

By the time John Leivers had moved to the Haggs his family was probably complete. He had married Alice Freeman Smith in Greasley parish church on the 9th December 1776 and by 1800 eleven children had been born to the couple. However by the time John made his will in 1814, there appeared to be only four survivors: — sons George, William and Joseph and daughter Elizabeth.

In the will John left all his personal estate and the possession and tenant right of the farm to his wife Alice for her lifetime and then to his son Joseph. The bequest of the tenancy of the farm was not binding since John was a tenant at will, and the landlord could have ended the tenancy at any time. (However the Melbourne estate records suggest that in most cases tenancies remained within the family, although rents were usually raised when the new tenant succeeded.) Monetary bequests of £5 were made to the three other surviving children and a similar amount was to be shared between two grandchildren. To his grandson John, son of his dead son of that name, was left a 24-gauge stocking frame.

This particular bequest is evidence that framework knitting was probably carried on by the small farmers in the area. The holding at the Haggs was never large enough to support more than subsistence farming and throughout the Leivers tenancy supplementary occupations were carried on by family members — initially framework-knitting and later coal mining.

After the elder John's death in 1821, Alice was granted the tenancy of the farm and remained tenant until January 1837, when she was buried in Greasley churchyard at the age of 79.

Alice was succeeded as tenant by son Joseph, who was paying £16/9/- by way of rent six months after being granted possession. Joseph had married Elizabeth Wharmby at Selston church on 16 May 1815 with his older brother William acting as one of the witnesses. The first of Joseph and Elizabeth's thirteen children was baptised in Greasley parish church within three months of the marriage but died within a month. Other children followed every two or three years until 1834 when there was an interval of five years before the last two children were born in 1839 and 1840.

Eight of Joseph and Elizabeth's children were baptised in non-conformist chapels — seven of them in the Independent chapel at nearby Moorgreen and the associated establishment at Ilkeston in Derbyshire. Whilst the last two children were baptised according to Anglican rites in the parish church, this association with non-conformity was to remain strong with the Haggs family until well into the twentieth century, latterly through membership of the Baptist chapel in Bagthorpe. Joseph and Elizabeth shared their adherence to the Independent denomination with the Anthony family who lived in the adjoining farm cottage.

Joseph Leivers was described as a labourer in the various baptismal records from 1818 to 1831. In the 1841 census he is recorded as a coal miner, as he was when his son John married in 1844. This could well have been at Willey colliery, which was located a few hundred yards from the Haggs at the other side of Willey Spring wood. In later censuses Joseph is recorded as a cottager and farm labourer (1851) and as a farmer (1861) which is also the occupation shown on his death certificate in 1865. These varying occupational descriptions reinforce the opinion that the Haggs tenants needed to undertake subsidiary employment in order to make ends meet, with the small acreage of the farm unable to provide a living for much of the time. So it seems likely that Joseph perhaps worked as an employee during the months when his smallholding required little attention — at least until his later years when son John's employment as a miner would bring additional income into the farm.

Joseph died on 1st of July 1865 aged 73 with his widow Elizabeth surviving him for 12 years, dying on 6 May 1877 at the age of 83.

Estate records give no indication that Joseph's tenancy was marked by particular events. It was during the period of his son John's tenancy that the Haggs was affected by major change, resulting from the enclosures of the commons in the adjoining parish of Selston. It is to John's life at the Haggs that we now turn.

John married Selina Henshaw at Greasley church in September 1844 a week after his 23rd birthday and was described as a coal miner. Selina was under 21 and was the only daughter of Rowland Henshaw, a coal miner from Brinsley, and his wife Sarah. The couple had moved to Brinsley by 1821 and Selina was born there sometime between 1823 and 1825. Seven children were born to John and Selina between 1845 and 1858. Two of the first three children born died in infancy, but the others seem to have survived until adulthood. John was recorded as a coal miner in the census returns of 1851 and 1861 but after the death of his father in 1865 took over the tenancy of the farm. The family's income continued to be supplemented by the usual pattern of the sons working in the collieries; the 1871 census records both Joseph, now married with two young children, and the 14 year-old Thomas both employed as miners. By 1881 Joseph had moved away from the farm, but Thomas stayed at the Haggs with his growing family until his father gave up the tenancy in 1898.

By 1881 John had increased his holding from 19 to 27 acres which was the result of the allocation of some of the former common lands in the neighbouring parish of Selston. It was John's rental of these fields, and the family's link with Henry Granger, the parish pinder and estate gamekeeper (son Joseph's father-in-law) that caused John to become involved in the disputes arising from the Selston enclosures. A brief description of those events is necessary to understand John's part in the troubles.

The parliamentary act authorising the enclosure of the wastes and commons in Selston (some 800 acres) was passed in 1865 but it was not until 1877, when fences were erected on the common land — most of which had been allocated to the major landlords — that things came to a head in the parish. The local committee of the Commons Protection League enlisted the help of the 'Commoners Champion' John de Morgan who addressed protest meetings near the Brick and Tile public house in Underwood in the summer of 1877 which were reported to have attracted crowds of 5000 people. The commoners claimed that every cottager 'has been in the habit of putting out one horse, or one cow, or six sheep or as many geese as he pleased' on to the commons.

This claim was flatly denied by the landowners and the Manor rules published in 1848 clearly stated that the inhabitants of cottages on the wastes or commons had no rights of pasture. In September, the protesters took direct action and some eight miles of fencing was torn up, hedges burned and crops destroyed. This action resulted in the arrest and trial of the 'Selston 26', seventeen of whom were found guilty of riot. De Morgan and William Peach, the local leader of the commoners, were jailed for several months having breached an earlier court injunction.

John Leivers and Henry Granger became joint tenants of two areas of former common land, one piece near Granger's cottage on Sandhills Road, the other being Brickyard Close which bordered the main road to Mansfield. The details of the lease confirm John's illiteracy — he marked the document after it had been read over to him. Both pieces of land were the subject of further protests which were reported in the local press. On three successive days in June 1878 protesters entered the Sandhills allotment and refused to leave. Granger and Leivers subsequently claimed damages for the trespass, and the ultimate outcome was a Chancery hearing and the imprisonment of one of the alleged ringleaders, William Stoppard. Within a couple of weeks more trouble flared up at Brickyard Close. On the morning of 8 July Granger found part of the fence knocked down and 25 beasts and 40 sheep in the field. Since the pinfold was not large enough to hold this number, Granger drove the impounded animals into a field at Haggs Farm. That evening over 100 men went to the field, broke open the gate and prepared to release the animals. Despite the presence of two policemen they pushed Leivers and Granger into a ditch. This scuffle resulted in further court proceedings with nine defendants being fined two guineas each for pound breach.[3]

John finally gave up the tenancy of the farm in 1898 and moved into Underwood. By the end of the following year he had died, being buried in Underwood churchyard on the 20th November 1899. So ended the association of the Leivers family and Haggs Farm. From now on the family's life was centered on the hamlets of Underwood and Bagthorpe and was to be dominated by coal mining for the next two generations.

The Anthony Tenancies

James Anthony is a rather shadowy figure. He is probably the man who married Martha Brown at Heanor in 1773. Six children of this marriage were baptised at Greasley church between 1777 and 1796 and so, as with John and Alice Leivers, it is probable that the family was complete by the time the Anthonys moved into their part of the old Haggs buildings.

By 1817 the tenancy had passed to son Samuel who was then 36 years old and he and his wife Susannah had already produced the first six of their eleven children. Their first child, Samuel was baptised at Kirkby in Ashfield in 1801 but by 1809 they were back in Greasley parish, probably at the Haggs, for two years later the baptism of son William confirms that the couple were residing there. Census returns provide a little more detail about Samuel. Successive returns from 1841 record that he was a farmer or cottager and confirm that between 1851 and 1861 his holding increased from 10 to 17 acres. On the occasion of his daughter Ruth's marriage in 1846 his occupation is given as thatcher which suggests that, like the Leivers tenants, Samuel needed to supplement his living from the farm by doing other work. It is certainly the case that at least his part of the old homestead was still thatched in 1879.

Susannah died in November 1860 and Samuel only outlived her by three and a half years dying on 6 May 1864 at the age of 83. In his will he appointed Thomas Barber of Lamb Close as one of the two executors, perhaps a further confirmation of his nonconformity since Barber was the minister and treasurer of Bagthorpe Baptist chapel in 1851.

After Samuel's death the tenancy passed to George Turner who was the second husband of Samuel's daughter Mary Ann. Turner was tenant from 1866 to May 1879 and during his tenancy instructions were given by the estate bailiff for the repainting of the cottage and for the re-thatching of house and cowshed.

The 1871 census shows Turner as a 72 year old shoemaker, with wife Mary Ann aged 49, two teenage sons of Mary Ann's first marriage and a nine year old servant girl.

But by 1879 the long association of the Anthony family with the Haggs had come to an end after some 70 odd years with the death of George Turner in January of that year. The end of that tenancy also saw a major change to the old homestead. The Anthony part was abandoned as living quarters and turned into outbuildings, with a new cottage being built for the incoming tenant John Whittaker.

The Chambers Years

There were six applications for the tenancy of Old Haggs when John Leivers moved out in 1898. The successful candidate was Edmund Chambers of Breach Road, Eastwood and it was during his tenancy, which lasted until 1910, that the farm's association with D.H. Lawrence developed.

Edmund Chambers had been born on Breach Road in 1863 where both his father Jonathon and grandfather William had been in business as grocers and pawnbrokers. Edmund's first job appears to have been as a grocery assistant in Nottingham — the 1881 census records him as an 18 year old employed as a provision merchant's assistant. This was at Burtons on Smithy Row, the most high-class grocers in Nottingham. By the end of that year (on 4th December) Edmund had married Sarah Ann Oates, a 22 year old lace hand who at the date of the census had been living with her parents David and Jane at Ortzen Street, Nottingham. On the marriage certificate, Edmund is described as a provision merchant and his father Jonathon as a gentleman!

The first two children of the marriage, Alan and May, were born in Nottingham in 1882 and 1883 but by the time daughter Jessie was born in January 1887 the family had moved to Netherfield on the eastern fringes of the city where Edmund was running a grocer's shop. In 1890 the family was in Caythorpe but the stay there was short-lived for the 1891 census shows Edmund back in Eastwood living on the Breach near his widowed mother Elizabeth who was still running the grocery store. Edmund's occupation is recorded as general labourer but at some time before the move to the Haggs he had established a milk round in Eastwood. It was with financial support from his mother that he began farming 'in a haphazard, happy go lucky sort of way' according to his son David. One other surviving child was born to the couple in Eastwood (Molly in 1895) so at the time of the move into the farmhouse the family comprised Edmund and Sarah with six children — Alan, May, Jessie, Hubert, Bernard and Molly. The family was to be completed some six months after the move to the Haggs by the birth on 13 October of Jonathan David, named after his grandfathers. From a rental probably dated shortly

The family in 1899

after Edmund had taken on the tenancy he is shown as holding just over 20 acres in Greasley, a little more than the final Leivers' holding in that parish. This additional land may have been the two fields across from Greasley church where Lawrence helped with the haymaking.

Estate records suggest that Edmund continued to be somewhat unsettled as regards his livelihood. He allegedly complained that the farm was over-run with rabbits and in 1903 gave notice to quit though this was subsequently withdrawn. At around the same time he applied again for the tenancy of two other farms on the estate. Towards the end of 1903 he had written to the Melbourne agent complaining about the rent relative to the quality of the land, and asking for the replacement of the kitchen copper which Sarah judged to be 'worn through'.

Thereafter he settled down for some years but finally gave up the tenancy in the first half of 1910 and moved to a farm at Woodthorpe on the outskirts of Nottingham. The story of the Chambers after their departure from the Haggs is the subject of another chapter.

The younger Chambers children attended Underwood school and the school log books provide some information about the family. In 1902 Jessie, aged 15, is recorded as a monitress in the mixed school; in November of that year she is listed as a pupil teacher under the headmaster George Stringfellow. She obviously found her duties stressful, for two months later the Head noted that 'Miss Chambers obliged to go home ill through being overworked with a large Standard III'.[4] In October 1903 Jessie transferred to the infants school because of overwork.

She appeared to find life easier there and was able to make good progress with her own studies for by May 1906 she had passed the King's Scholarship examination. In the autumn of that year she returned to the mixed school where she remained until December 1909, leaving to take a better paid post at West Bridgford.

The story of D.H. Lawrence's association with the Chambers family, and Jessie in particular, has been told many times — by a host of Lawrence biographers, by Jessie herself in *A Personal Record*, by her brother David, and in fictional guise by Lawrence himself, primarily in *Sons and Lovers*. The subject is dealt with in this book in later chapters.

Underwood school staff in 1907. Jessie Chambers is in the middle of the front row

24

Tenants of Old Haggs after the Chambers

Because of the lack of access to the Barber estate records, our information after 1916 when they bought the farm, is limited to odd items apart from trade directories and electoral registers. These enable us to compile a fairly accurate list of the later tenants but the detail of their life at the farm is almost totally unknown.

When Edmund Chambers gave up his tenancy there was again no shortage of applications for the farm — seven on this occasion. The successful applicant was George Ward from Lockington near Derby, who was to remain at the Haggs until his death in 1935, becoming a tenant of the Barbers after the property was included in their purchase of the farms and land surrounding their home at Lamb Close in 1916.

But we have a brief insight into the Ward family from the recollections of Annie Granger, their neighbour at New Haggs. Annie was a close friend of the Ward daughters of whom Edith went to be ladies-maid to Miss Joan Barber at Lamb Close, and Hilda went to work at another farm. Annie recalled that 'Mr Ward used to carry milk to Underwood in pails on a yoke.'

Ward was replaced as tenant by William Fry. In his return for the National farm survey of 1941, Fry stated that he had been tenant for six years and was currently paying rent of £64. He had no help on the farm, nor any motive power. But the same month Fry gave up the tenancy, reportedly persuaded to do so because of the neglected state of the farm. He was followed as tenant by Albert Rigley (and wife Maud). From a report in 1942 Rigley appeared to be in some need of guidance as regards improving the rundown and weed-infested farm he had taken over. The farmhouse was said to be in fair condition but the outbuildings were in a bad state. There was now a piped water supply — previously water had to be drawn from the spring in Willey Wood — but no electricity. Like his predecessor, Rigley is reputed to have relied on horse power to perform his ploughing.

After some years in the old farmhouse, the Rigleys moved into New Haggs cottage and Mrs Rigley's father and mother — Frank and Lily Wilson — became the final tenants of the old farm. This was probably around 1946–47 since the first reference to the Wilsons in the electoral registers was in 1947. The Wilsons lived rent free in the old farmhouse until Frank Wilson died in April 1963 at the age of 81. These final tenants of the old farmhouse are

shown in the photograph taken on David Chambers' visit to the farm around 1954–55.

In January 1964 David Chambers wrote 'The Haggs looks tired and decayed now; it may even fall down.' Two years later he mounted a campaign to secure the future of the buildings, giving interviews on local radio and received support from various local preservation and historical organisations. A letter in the *Guardian* in July 1966, signed by various prominent literary figures including Alan Sillitoe, Rebecca West and David Garnett, asserted that the threat of dilapidation and possible demolition would be a 'literary tragedy.' The upshot of the campaign was that both Old and New Haggs were scheduled as Grade II listed buildings.

The Tenants of New Haggs

In May 1879 Fox, the Melbourne estate agent, wrote to Earl Cowper as follows:-

> I have let the place (the old Anthony tenancy) to a very thriving industrious man named Whittaker. The rent of the house is at present £12 per annum. It was intended to repair the old house ... at a cost of £80 but on stripping the thatch we find the place so bad that it will be much better to (convert) it into outbuildings for stock which are much wanted at a cost of £20 to £30 and to build a new cottage

at a cost of about £150. As these premises will accommodate about 20 acres of the adjoining common ... this would be a judicious outlay and I shall be glad to have your Lordship's sanction of it.

Earl Cowper gave approval within a cost limit of £150 although the estate account books show the actual cost of building work totalled £255/19/6d.

John Whittaker remained at New Haggs until his death in 1892 at the age of 73.

There appeared to have been only one applicant for the vacant tenancy — William Pearson of Lodge Farm, Newthorpe, where according to the 1881 census he was farming 84 acres. However it seems that Pearson may have applied on behalf of his son, for it is William junior who appears in the 1901 census return for the Haggs.

This shows that William junior and his wife Elizabeth had lived for a short time at East Bridgford where their eldest child was born in 1890; five more children were to be born at the Haggs between 1893 and 1904. The first of the children born at the Haggs, daughter Betsy, became a monitress at Underwood school and appears in the staff photograph sitting on Jessie Chambers' right.

The Pearsons were to remain at New Haggs until 1916 and the documents relating to the Barber purchase in that year show that William was renting four fields in Selston parish, totalling some 19 acres and another 14 acres in Greasley.

The reason for the Pearsons departure from the Haggs is not known, but their replacement as tenant was a family relation — Albert Henry Granger, a cousin of William Pearson. Albert had previously been a publican and was about 33 years old when he moved into New Haggs with wife Gertrude and daughter Annie Rebecca. The family had an unhappy start to life there, for in October 1917 Gertrude died at the early age of 36, thought to be due to tuberculosis. Albert later remarried and a daughter of this marriage was born in 1920.

Daughter Annie recalled that life at the farm was hard work for many relatives came to stay for long periods. Every day she had to fetch 16 pails of water for the cattle from the spring in Willey Wood; her father delivered milk around Underwood in his horse and cart. The Grangers stayed at the Haggs until around 1936 when Albert returned to the licensed trade as publican at the Robin Hood in Brinsley.

Horace Whitehead then took over the tenancy and was tenant at the time of the National Farm Survey in 1941 which shows him renting 41 acres at a rent of £64. Details of the final tenants are sparse, mainly coming from electoral registers. These show that a Henry Clay was tenant in 1945, but a year later Albert Maggs was the recorded occupier. It seems that it was on his departure that the Rigleys moved into New Haggs from the old farmhouse, staying there until Mr Rigley's death in 1979.

Description of Old Haggs

Various plans in the estate papers during the period of John Leivers' tenancy illustrate the layout of the old farm. When these are matched with photographs of the buildings in the 20th century and descriptions by Jessie and David Chambers and D.H. Lawrence it is possible to provide a reasonably clear description of the farm. The farmhouse had two living rooms — a kitchen and parlour according to a plan of 1876, the first around 16ft × 12ft, the parlour about 12ft square. (A later plan in the time of the Chambers shows the parlour somewhat larger than the kitchen/house.) Behind the living quarters were dairies and scullery. Adjoining the house were a stable and barn; until 1879 the Anthony house abutted the parlour. The farm had four bedrooms, two above the living quarters, two above the stable and barn. A piggery, cowshed and second barn were at the front of the house with a stackyard and an orchard across the track which led from the farm to Felley Mill Lane and Underwood. The house faced west towards Willey Spring Wood; a garden lay behind the stable and barn looking down towards Felley Farm.

Jessie Chambers described the house as follows:

> The house was long, and the line of the roof was broken by a gable window which matched the porch over the front door. The farm buildings adjoined the house and formed one side of a square. The front garden lay snugly in the angle between the house and our neighbour's high yard-wall and buildings. From the front door we looked down the length of garden which was fenced off from the crew-yard, over a croft and into the wood which shut us in completely on the west ... at the back of the house was a big garden divided from the stockyard by railings, containing two fine cherry trees with a low spreading apple tree between them, several plum trees, and currant and gooseberry bushes. Beyond was a rough grass plot with an apple tree in the centre and clumps of daffodils in the hedgebottom. From the stackyard the land dipped to the valley where we could see in the hollow the red

roofs of Felley Mill, and away on the right Moorgreen reservoir gleaming like tarnished silver.[5]

The Haggs Today

Old Haggs has now been uninhabited for some 50 years and the new cottage for at least half that period. Their status as Grade II listed buildings provided some limited protection but at the time Clive Leivers first wrote this passage the local authority no longer carried out regular inspections of the properties to ensure they were maintained in reasonable repair. In more recent years inspections by Nottinghamshire County Council Historic Buildings Department have resumed with the most recent being in 2022. This found that Haggs Farm, although still standing, urgently needed ventilation to stop damp and rot. As a recent photography shows, the Old Haggs, though standing and reportedly wind and weatherproof, is but a shadow of the living home and farm it used to be.

The owners remain opposed to any form of public access. However, some recent contacts have been established with the owners by Haggs Farm Preservation Society through the agency of Nottinghamshire County Council and it is hoped that some more substantive managed access arrangements may be possible in the future, even if not full public access.

In the meantime, the visitor to Lawrence's 'country of my heart' has to settle for a distant view from public footpaths in the neighbouring countryside. However, such a walk still provides some insight into why the farm and its locality had such an impact on the young Lawrence.

Notes

1   Nottinghamshire Archives DDLM series
2   Nottinghamshire Archives PRNW
3   Eagle and Heath, 'Selston and the enclosure of its common lands' *Transactions of the Thoroton Society* Vol. 90 64–68.
    Nottinghamshire Guardian 12 August 1878
4   Nottinghamshire Archives, Underwood school log books SIL 147/5
5   ET 21–22

Chapter 2
Memories of D.H. Lawrence
Jonathan David Chambers

This is the text of a lecture given by Professor Chambers on several occasions to a variety of audiences. It was first published in Renaissance and Modern Studies *and is used here with the permission of his daughter Ann Howard.*

D.H. Lawrence has been described by E.M. Forster as 'the greatest imaginative writer of our generation'. To undertake to speak on a figure of such eminence is not only a privilege but a great responsibility. I should, of course, say that I am speaking not about his literary work or his standing in the world of letters. I have no qualification to do that. I cannot even pretend to be thoroughly acquainted with — or even an ardent admirer of — the whole of his works. His poetry, yes; his letters and essays and his early novels, *The White Peacock* and *Sons and Lovers;* but neither his long novels nor his sociological works are to my taste. I propose therefore to speak of him simply as I knew him during the years when he visited my family at the Haggs and when he played such a vital role in our lives. He certainly made my own life a great deal more exciting than it would have otherwise been, and I can honestly say that, as a child, I had great affection for him. He brought an infectious zest for life and a vitality that inspired everybody he met; life became more exciting with him and he left an impression on us all that can never be erased. It is on the memories of those days that I shall mainly draw in this lecture.

But besides my own memories, and not always to be distinguished from them, are the memoirs of my two sisters, Jessie and May. Many of you will know the memoir entitled *D.H. Lawrence: a Personal Record* which my sister Jessie wrote of those years in 1935. It is vividly written with all the emotional intensity which she brought to everything she did, and is recognised as an indispensable source for this period of Lawrence's life. There is also a memoir written by my sister May which I found in a box of her papers deposited with my brother in Saskatchewan where she lived as a schoolmistress for many years. It throws valuable light on Lawrence as a schoolboy and on the relations between his mother and father which played such an important part in his life. I handed the manuscript over to Edward Nehls who was at that time completing his *Composite Biography of D.H. Lawrence* and he included it in Volume 3 of his works in the section entitled 'The Chambers Papers'.

I think you may well ask how did it come about that I and other members of my family were in the position to speak or write with such intimacy of these years of Lawrence's life? The answer is that we lived in the same small mining town of Eastwood and were, for some years, almost neighbours. The two families, the Lawrences and the Chambers, were old established Eastwood families and both occupied houses — though at different times — in the same street known as the Breach. By the time we reached the Breach, however, the Lawrences had moved up the hill to Walker Street and later to Lynncroft. This is important because the houses up the hill were felt to be superior to those in the Breach; and the one on Lyncroft was semi-detached with a bay window and its own entry. The Lawrences were moving up in the world and were very conscious of the fact.

The contact between the two families, however, remained close. It existed on two levels; on the level of the children going to the local schools and playing together in the field and along the brookside that separated the Breach from Walker Street; and secondly it existed on the level of the Chapel or the 'Congo' as my brothers irreverently called it, where the two families met on Sunday and at other times. It was especially the meeting place of the two mothers. They were both strangers to the colliery community and they found in the Chapel a degree of culture that was otherwise entirely lacking in their lives; this was the only place in which they felt really at home in an otherwise alien world. It is difficult for us to realise today what the Chapel way of life meant to the more sensitive and refined members of a colliery village. It imposed upon them, of course, a rigid puritan morality, but this represented no sacrifice on their part as it was the only rule of life they knew and was part of the air they breathed. In addition, meeting at the Chapel enabled the two mothers to exchange confidences and share their troubles, and they had much to talk about; they both hated the mining community to which their husbands had brought them. My mother was rather frightened of it: she had never before seen men coming home black from head to foot with coaldust and dreaded to hear their rough loud voices and strange dialect, and their heavy boots dragging along the pavement. Mrs Lawrence wasn't frightened; I cannot believe she was frightened of anything; she just despised and hated them and blamed herself for allowing herself to be brought among them. Perhaps especially she blamed her husband who had, she felt, lured her by false pretences into this trap.

This is an important aspect of Lawrence's life. And I think it is worth a moment's notice. How did it come about that this refined and relatively well-educated woman should be brought into the heart of a mining community and to have to spend her life rueing the consequences?

I will tell the story as I heard it from my father when I was very young. At the time of the marriage Arthur Lawrence, the father, was a collier, very skilled, and highly respected and already a butty, which represented the climax of the average collier's ambitions. He was also an attractive character, lively and gay, with an infectious laugh and a good singing voice; the life and soul of any company of which he was a member. I think there is no doubt that D.H. Lawrence acquired some of his most attractive characteristics, perhaps particularly his inexhaustible zest for life, from his father and also at least one of his accomplishments. It was from his father that he learned to dance. Arthur Lawrence was a keen dancer and it was as a result of a meeting in a dance hall in Nottingham that he met his future wife, Lydia Beardsall. We should remember that he was an attractive young man, with dancing blue eyes, a long black curly beard, and a lively talker, of course in the Eastwood dialect. Lydia Beardsall was also a clever and attractive woman, trained as a teacher and lately jilted by a schoolmaster. They were drawn to one another from the first encounter, and he soon asked her to marry him. When she asked him what he did for a living he said he was a contractor. Now that was strictly true. He contracted to get coal from an area called a stall; he employed and paid his own workmen and sold the coal to the Barber and Walker Company. I should mention that a butty's pay varied according to the kind of stall he worked. If the coal was difficult to get, he might have little to draw after paying his men (and Arthur Lawrence's stalls were often difficult as he was usually on bad terms with the managers). But when the going was good his pay packet could be substantial. But of course he worked down the pit and came home black. When he came home the first day after the wedding his wife scarcely knew him; when he sat down in his black to the meal she had prepared for him she was shocked; and when it came to bathing in the 'dolly tub' in front of the fire her cup was full. It was traditionally a miner's wife's task to wash her husband's back, a necessary task since the coal dust, congealed with sweat, stuck like lacquer to the skin; but it was a task that Mrs Lawrence regarded as humiliating and degrading. She never forgave him. She considered she had been basely betrayed; she had been lowered in her own eyes and she would punish him as she was well able to do. She had a tongue like a whiplash and laid about her with such effect that Arthur Lawrence eventually became almost a stranger in his own house. His real life outside the pit was spent at the pub and this happy, carefree collier lad was eventually reduced to little better than a drunken sot. She had indeed taken her revenge.

The effect of the deep division of the Lawrence household on the sensitive young boy growing up in it has been described in my sister May's memoir in a scene that is worth recalling. She was having tea with Mrs Lawrence and Bert, as we always called him, and Ada, his sister. As usual they were in a gay mood, with Bert amusing them with his vivacious chatter and brilliant mimicry. As my sister said, he was like a darting sunbeam bringing a glow of light into the little room. Then they heard the sound of his father's footsteps as he returned from work. Immediately there was silence. Bert hunched up his shoulders and glowered at his plate. Mr Lawrence talked gaily to the two girls, completely ignoring Bert and his mother. As soon as he left the table life returned to the little party, but the transformation in Bert Lawrence made by his father's presence, left an indelible impression on my sister's mind; she said he seemed to be transformed from a fairy prince into a poisonous toad.

This then was how our relations with the Lawrence family began. Two events now happened which might have been expected to open a gap between our two families. One, not perhaps a very important one in the circumstances, was the award of a County Scholarship for Lawrence to the Nottingham High School. Always an alien among the boys of Eastwood, he now became one apart, a mardy kid, in the language of his contemporaries. But a far more important event had already happened that might have been decisive in separating the two families. A year before the award of the scholarship we had moved to the Haggs, a little farm tucked away in the woods on the outer side of Moorgreen reservoir, three miles from Eastwood by road and rather more than two by field paths. To the great surprise of my family he came to see us one day, accompanied by his mother. It was a beautiful afternoon in late spring and the Haggs was looking at its best; and the best at the Haggs in those days was very good. The woods came almost up to the garden fence on one side; on another side they were a couple of fields away and behind, in the distance, rose the tree-lined ridge of the Annesley hills. The woods near the Haggs were carpeted in bluebells and lady smock and campions. There was a riot of colour and a chorus of birdsong, and all the familiar noises of a traditional farmyard.

To Lawrence, coming from the dreary streets of Eastwood, it was a fairyland. From that moment began the first phase of his love affair with the Haggs.

You will notice it was not a love affair with any person; it was a love affair with the place, the little farmhouse, clothed in Virginia creeper and honeysuckle, with its old mare, Flower, who leaned over the garden fence and nibbled the roses, the good-natured bull terrier Trip, who lay across the hearth in front of the fire, and the two massive old sows to whom he gave classical names. One, a cheerful chubby creature with twinkling blue eyes, always ready to hold up her snout for an apple, he called Dido; the other, a long, lean, lugubrious animal, always complaining and never satisfied, he called Circe. Whether this description fits the two classical personages I am not able to say, but I have always thought of them in that way ever since.

The only person with whom he had any close contact at that time was my eldest sister May, who was studying to be a teacher. He insisted — much against her will — on helping her with her homework, and dragging her out to the wood to pick flowers, and especially to look for rare specimens of which he seemed to have, even then, considerable knowledge; or they would search for a robin's nest in an old kettle, or stumble across a lark's nest in the hollow made by the feet of the farm animals in the soft clay, or a peewit's eggs on the stark surface after ploughing. But for the rest of my brothers and sisters he was still something of a stranger from another world. They were shy of this vivacious young man in his Eton clothes and with his impetuous manners.

But a third event happened that might well have brought our relationship with him to an end and silenced the strange story of Bert Lawrence for ever. On leaving the High School in 1901 he took a post in Nottingham as a clerk in a small factory making elastic bandages for medical purposes, but within a few weeks he went down with a serious attack of pneumonia. This was a very anxious time, especially for his mother. I remember, for by this time I can begin to call upon my own recollection of events, on my father's return from Eastwood where he delivered milk, our first question was about Bert and his mother. She had already lost an elder son, Ernest, for whom she had a passionate affection; and now her second favourite, Bert, was dangerously ill. We wondered what would happen to her if he also was taken. Fortunately the question did not need to be answered. One day my father returned with the news that Bert was getting better; then that he was already up. My father had seen him sitting on his mother's lap, with his long legs, that had grown while he lay in bed, hanging down almost to the floor. My father suggested that, in a few days, when he got stronger, he could ride up in the milk cart and join his lads in the hayfield.

The invitation was accepted. Then began the second phase of the love affair with the Haggs. It lasted about six years from 1902 to 1908. During that time he was training as a teacher, at Beauvale school as a pupil teacher, as a part-time student at the Ilkeston Teachers' Training Centre, and then at University College, Nottingham. During the whole of that period he came to see us constantly, at least once a week, sometimes oftener, and always at holiday times, and especially at Christmas. Then he was the leader of our festivities, searching the woods for holly and organising Christmas games which we scarcely hear of now — Consequences, Family Coach, and especially Charades. He was a welcome guest. His vitality seemed to illumine the house and stimulate the entire household. He had what might be called an electric presence, raising the potential of everyone around him. As for me, I adored him. I looked for his coming at weekends and I could not imagine a Christmas without him. I think everyone loved him at this time; he combined with his vivacity a sweetness of disposition that was quite irresistible. There were high words sometimes between him and my brothers on the subject of the mushrooms which they found together, but which he claimed because he could run faster to pick them up. He wanted them for his father's tea, he said; an interesting admission that he wasn't always on bad terms with his father. And there were flashes of temper which showed the fires that were later to break out so fiercely. I remember in particular an incident in which one of my brothers, probably having grown tired of hearing young Lawrence expatiating on the beauty of the bluebells, chose to throw himself down and roll among a bed where they were thickset. Lawrence, in a rage, chased him on his long legs and knocked him flat on the ground. But that was a mere flash of lightning in a summer's sky. The mood passed and the incident was forgotten. He fitted into our family circle as though he had been born into it. My mother loved to see him coming up the garden path, bringing an air of irrepressible youth with him. He was not only a gay and artless companion, he was also a great help. He set about household tasks, such as cooking and even washing, and would help to prepare the family meal and lay the table. With Bert in charge, the meal was a family party. There were seven of us — I had three sisters and three brothers — besides my parents and Lawrence and possibly a friend or his sister Ada to get round the table in that tiny kitchen. Tempers could easily have become frayed, but with Lawrence there everything went with a sweetness and gaiety that is difficult to convey. He saw to it that such delicacies as stewed prunes and apricots, and tinned salmon, were fairly apportioned among a rather obstreperous growing family, including myself, a vociferous little heathen, anxious not to be forgotten.

After the meal the table would be cleared, then the fun began. He taught us to dance, especially the waltz and the polka, which it is interesting again to note, he had learned from his father, and above all to sing. He brought copies of part songs from school and made us all learn our parts. He even went into the cowshed to practise my eldest brother in singing the tenor parts while he was milking. Lawrence himself had no sort of singing voice: it was highpitched and liable to crack when he was excited; fortunately we all had voices and he made us use them. My father bought an ancient piano for these family concerts, but as none of us could play Lawrence persuaded his sister Ada, somewhat reluctantly, to come from time to time to play for us. He also introduced chess and cards and all the usual party games, but above all we played charades. Lawrence, of course, was the moving spirit; but everybody was brought in.

I remember he was especially fond of dressing up my brother Alan in some oriental costume, as an Arab chief or a Jewish prophet, and I can see him standing back and admiring my brother's display of tanned neck and arms. (They were good friends at the time and sometimes slept out under the haystacks.) He himself played many parts; one that stands out in my memory is when he played Pharoah, sitting on an improvised throne (my mother's rocking chair) on our parlour table. (I should have mentioned that for these games we used the kitchen as a dressing room and played our parts in the large, low room which we called the parlour.) I can hear him now responding to Moses (my brother Alan) begging humbly on behalf of the Israelites, his voice rising to a shriek, screaming that he would never let the children of Israel go. Another time he was a coachman, again on the parlour table, jumping up to whip his horses and crashing my father's tall hat on the low ceiling over his ears. My own greatest triumph was when both sides decided to put on a funeral scene, and I played the part of the corpse in both. I had nothing to do, I could take a central part and see and hear everything. What could be more delightful? And then we would sing — Scots Wha Hae, Starboard Watch, Tavern in the Town, and a dozen other songs. And when it was all over, and it was time to set off on his dark two mile walk to Eastwood, we would gather round the kitchen door and send him off with a chorus that echoed and re-echoed through the silent woods. It was a long and dark and often very muddy walk; through the farmyard, then through two fields, and down to the Warren — a plantation of dark fir trees — and on to Moorgreen reservoir and along Engine Lane to Eastwood. Sometimes we gave him a hurricane lamp to light his way, and when the mud was particularly deep and wet my mother tied paper round his ankles to protect him.

He was trespassing most of the way, of course, but the keepers never molested him. Perhaps I should stop here for a moment to mention the question of gamekeepers. We all regarded them as our natural enemies. We children were very frightened of them, though they never gave us any real cause. They were certainly not as fierce then as they are now. Lawrence had only one brush with them as far as I know. This happened when he and his friends decided they must explore the shooting box in the middle of High Park Wood. This was the holy of holies of the keepers, the headquarters where guests of the landowner met for the periodical shoots. The keeper found Lawrence and his friends peeping through the windows and ordered them off. There were high words; Lawrence was white with fury, but as far as I know no blows were exchanged. But the figure of the keeper left an indelible mark on all our minds, and has a peculiar significance in Lawrence's work.

But if those wonderful Christmas parties were the highlights of our winter evenings, there were equally bright days in summer, especially at hay-making time. We had two large fields two miles away at Greasley, and it was a great day when we rumbled along with horses and carts and all the paraphernalia of old-fashioned hay-making; and as far as I can remember the weather was always fine and sunny. If Lawrence was on holiday he worked all day in the fields; at other times he came after school and soon the news went round that the Chambers were hay-making at Greasley, and Bert Lawrence was there. First one and then another of his friends — girlfriends for the most part — would join us, and it seems to me, looking back, that the field was full of girls in their summer frocks going through the motions of getting in the hay. Then baskets of fruit would be opened, and cakes and tarts spread on the grass, and in no time there was a picnic; then singing and perhaps a dance on the grass. Then my father would say, 'Come on now, let's get on with some work' and everybody would set to with a will to make up for lost time.

Perhaps you will wonder, with all those girls about, whether that was all that happened. I would like to assure you that it was. Lawrence had flocks of girls around him wherever he went; he went shopping with them, and helped them to choose their hats and frocks; they went long walks together, over the Misk hills and through Annesley Park, or they took a train into Derbyshire to Ambergate and explored Wingfield Manor, but I am sure that nothing by the way of love-making took place. We should remember we were still a puritan society and Lawrence, like everybody else, was part of it. In the whole of the period I knew him I never saw him kiss, or attempt to kiss, anyone.

But alongside this gaiety and high spirits there was deep and serious reading being done. Books from the Mechanics Library at Eastwood flowed through the house, and floods of talk about their authors; Hardy, Bennett, Wells, Shaw, Huxley, Darwin, Conrad; and foreign names too. Anatole France, Dostoevsky, Tolstoy and Turgenev, a mysterious German philosopher, Schopenhauer, and I think Nietzsche; and a book of poetry that everyone seemed to know something about — the *Golden Treasury*.

Of course, at that time, not only Lawrence but my sister Jessie was reading these books. She, like him, was studying to become a teacher; three days a week at the Underwood village school and two days at the Ilkeston Centre. To get there she had to walk three miles or more to Langley Mill station to catch a train, and back again at night, and then do her homework in the evening. I mention this to show how determined she was to break away from the drudgery of the farm kitchen and make her escape into the world of books where her imagination could expand. She had a passion for poetry and went about the house and on the way from school reciting especially the poems of Scott — *Marmion, The Lay of the Last Minstrel;* and also Wordsworth. She recited *Lucy Gray* to me with a tragic intensity which I have never forgotten. I could see those footsteps in the snow and their disappearance over the broken ridge and I often wished we could have something more cheerful.

Of course, Lawrence found an ideal companion in her. She learned all he could teach her, but I think she gave something in return. She had as deep an appreciation of the beauty of nature and the nuances of language as he, and her emotional experience of them was, if anything, more intense. Though intellectually she was his inferior, in emotional depth she was his equal. She realised his genius and helped him by her sympathetic understanding to realise it himself. She did this in a practical way, too. She found some poems written on scraps of paper and on the backs of envelopes. She collected and copied them and sent them up to the editor of the *English Review.* The result was an invitation to London to see Ford Madox Hueffer, Violet Hunt, and other literary figures, a visit that marked the launching of Lawrence into the literary world. Of course, she was in love with him. They were so much together that people thought they were engaged, or soon would become so, but it was not to be. The reasons for this were, I think, the bitter, unsleeping jealousy and the possessiveness of his mother, who hated to see him so involved in our family circle and especially in his relations with Jessie. She had a subtle way of reminding her son of this. She used to leave the candle burning in her room at night until he came home, and he went to bed with the unpleasant reminder that he had kept his mother awake by staying so late at the Haggs. He loved his mother and was grieved that he should cause her unhappiness; but he also loved the Haggs. Whether he loved Jessie is another matter; I think he felt her necessary to him in his development as an artist, but I think he feared her, too; he was afraid of being absorbed in her over-powering personality, and was defeated by her ingrained puritanism. He instinctively felt that marriage with her would have been disastrous; and he was right. My mother certainly thought it would be a mistake; she said that she would sooner see her daughter in her grave than married to Lawrence. But they continued to be close friends and to work together, even after he became engaged to Louie Burrows.

There were other signs of change in Lawrence at this time. He was finishing his course at the University College. He was 22 and not able to earn enough to keep himself. He was becoming impatient with the narrow life of Eastwood. Above all, he was breaking the bonds of Chapel religion and Chapel morality. This seems to me a very important turning point between the old life and the new, and I think I can identify the occasion of it, although I cannot be sure of the date. We were returning from Chapel on a summer evening; his mother, my mother, various members of the family, with Lawrence and perhaps one or two of his friends. It was a beautiful evening, and we chose to return through the field paths and through the Warren. Lawrence was in a dark mood and by the time we had reached the Warren he began to inveigh against the Chapel and all it stood for and especially against the minister, the Reverend Robert Reid, for whom we all had a great respect. Lawrence poured a stream of scorn and raillery upon the poor man, made fun of his ideas, and mimicked his way of expressing them; it was a fierce, uncontrollable tirade, an outpouring of long pent-up rage that left us all silent and rather frightened. We had never seen him in such a mood before. He seemed to be beside himself. His mother was as shocked as the rest of us, and perhaps she had the most reason. It was she who had fastened the Chapel bonds around him; he submitted, but with a bad grace. He told his friend, Mrs Collishaw, that he hated the Chapel, even as a boy, and only went to please his mother. He was now in open rebellion. He was giving notice to his mother that the days of her reign over him, at least in this respect, were numbered.

There were other examples of the conflict that was raging in him. I remember, on one of our many visits to Felley Mill, he leapt backwards and forwards again and again over the mill race that flowed in a dark rush of water from the mill pond to the sluice below. It was a narrow channel, but it sloped down at a steep angle; and had he missed his footing he would have had a nasty fall in the swirling water. It is a dry ditch now and overgrown with brambles and looks harmless enough, but to my sister and me who watched him it seemed as though some demon possessed him and he was defying it to do its worst.

A second occasion was more sinister, illustrating a destructive streak in him that we had not suspected. My sister May had become engaged to a stonemason, Bill Holbrook. He was a highly-skilled workman and an exceedingly droll companion. He was, in his way, almost as entertaining as Lawrence himself, and I think Lawrence may have felt some jealousy that he should have to share our affections and admiration with this untutored workman. He was especially incensed when Bill produced two effigies which he had carved in May's honour. We were very proud of them, and set them up at either side of the garden gate. Lawrence thought they were hideous; he railed against them whenever he came, and finally, in a fit of temper, he picked up a large hammer and brought it down with a crash on each of them. They lay in ruins, and we silently swept up the pieces and resolved not to have the two young men at the house together at the same time.

These incidents marked the closing stages of Lawrence's association with the Haggs. He was busy on his first novel, *The White Peacock*. At the suggestion of my father he contributed three stories to the *Nottinghamshire Guardian*, one of which, published over my sister's name, earned him three guineas, the first money he ever received from his writing. He was also completing his teachers' training course and looking for a job. He had done brilliantly in his Certificate examination, and he said he would not take a job under £95 a year. He secured one at £95 a year at Croydon in the autumn of 1908. And in November 1908 he left Eastwood for London. He never came to the Haggs again.

There is one rather melancholy chapter to the Haggs story that must be mentioned. Soon after going to Croydon he began to write his autobiographical novel *Paul Morel*. He sent the opening chapter of the first draft to my sister, who advised a different approach. He accepted the advice, and the result was the first part of *Sons and Lovers* as we know it now. Other chapters followed, and my sister realised that the novel was taking a direction which, she believed, was untrue to the facts but, which was more important to her, was false to his real genius. She believed he had allowed the lower part of his nature to take command; she also saw that the book had put her in an entirely false light; and made it abundantly clear that the mother, Mrs Morel, had triumphed over Miriam. She felt bitterly about these things, and wrote to him, begging him to alter them. Instead, when the next batch of manuscripts arrived, she found that those aspects of the book that had given her the most pain were strengthened and underlined. This was a cruel blow; to read the manuscripts was a form of torment to her; and she wrote to her friend Helen Corke, 'if he doesn't soon let me alone he'll be the death of me.' She sent them back without comment; and the next letter that came she returned unopened. This episode raises the difficult question of what are the obligations of an artist to the human models on whom he places his characterization. For Lawrence, this was an irrelevant question. As he himself said, 'With should and ought I have nothing to do.' The artist should obey only his daemon.

So ended this idyllic friendship, so sacred but so full of anguish. He went on to follow his stormy path without her. She went on to make a happy marriage, but not before she herself had written her own version of the story in a novel entitled *Eunice Temple*. When the publisher to whom it was sent demurred at producing it on the grounds that, although it was a fine piece of writing, it would not be a commercial success, she burnt it, together with all the letters she had received from Lawrence. This ruthless self-abnegation was entirely in character, but it left a gap in the Morel-Miriam story that can never be filled. She lived an uneventful but happy life in correspondence with many literary figures. But the memory of the days of the Haggs was never far away. In 1930, when Lawrence was dying, a fact of which she was entirely ignorant, she declared that the kitchen where she was working was filled with an unearthly light, and she heard a voice, 'can you remember only the pain and none of the joy?' She was an intensely truthful woman and I must accept this as a part of her experience. In 1935 she produced *A Personal Record* and signed it E.T., the initials of Eunice Temple, the only link we have with the novel she had destroyed. She died of a brain haemorrhage in 1944.

Chapter 3
My first incentive to write
Clive Leivers

In his letter to Rolf Gardiner, Lawrence, looking back some 20 years, identified Haggs Farm as the place where he was first inspired to write.

The memoir of David Chambers in Chapter 2 tells of Lawrence's relationship with the Chambers family, the farm and its setting. This essay is an attempt to assess the importance of the Haggs, of its surroundings within what Lawrence called 'the country of my heart', and of the Chambers family in relation to Lawrence's work. It will consider his use of the surrounding countryside, his portrayal of individual members of the Chambers family and the practical help he received from Jessie in establishing himself as a writer.

The Countryside
In his essay *Nottingham and the Mining Countryside,* Lawrence describes the rural surroundings of Eastwood as 'an extremely beautiful countryside, just between the red sandstone and the oak trees of Nottingham and the cold limestone, the ash trees, the stone fences of Derbyshire ... To me, as a child and young man, it was still the old England of the forest and agricultural past.'[1] He then compares this to the ugliness of the colliery housing in 'those sordid and hideous Squares' of Eastwood, the place where he was born and where he lived until he was twenty-three years old.

Every critic and biographer writing about the life and work of Lawrence has stressed his deep knowledge and sympathy with the natural world and the significance of the landscape around Haggs Farm to his early work. Melvyn Bragg has described Lawrence as 'one of the greatest nature writers in the English language' and this claim is amply supported by his descriptions of the 'country of my heart.' In 1959 Mark Schorer wrote in *A D.H. Lawrence Miscellany*

> There is probably no other writer ... whose works respond so immediately to his geographical environment as Lawrence, and certainly there is no other modern writer to whose imagination *place* makes such a direct and intense appeal.

In that same collection of essays another American, Robert Gajdusek, noted that in Lawrence's first novel *The White Peacock,* set in the immediate vicinity of the Haggs, there is mention of 145 different trees, shrubs or plants, 51 animals and 40 birds; as one other commentator has said — 'Not (merely) mentioned (but) worked intimately into the round of the year in the Felley Mill valley'.[2]

Claude Sinzelle described the novel as 'a poem of nature' in which the natural scenes 'reveal a deep reverence for wild life.' Bridget Pugh commented on 'a quite extraordinary sensitivity of observation' and suggested that the most significant feature of this first novel 'is the evocation of the countryside around Eastwood' with 'the freshness of its natural detail.' Roy Spencer suggests that into *The White Peacock* Lawrence 'poured his deepest and most sensitive feelings about nature and wild things' with his ability to describe natural events showing 'a unique gift.[3]' More generally John Worthen describes how

> He drew so much on the place, that particular identifications are almost irrelevant. The landscape of his first novel *The White Peacock* is steeped in the countryside around the Haggs; the same woods and fields were the setting for his first poems, and then appeared in his stories *A Prelude, A Modern Lover, The Shades of Spring, A Fragment of Stained Glass, Second Best* and *Love Among the Haystacks.* Great stretches of *Sons and Lovers* drew upon that particular landscape ... it went on appearing long after Lawrence had left the Haggs, Eastwood and England; the wood in *Lady Chatterley* is in almost every way a recreation of the wood, with the same keepers' hut he had seen that day in 1901.[4]

And it is on the final page of the second version of *Lady Chatterley's Lover,* written in 1926/7, that Lawrence gives Haggs Farm its real name for the only time in his fiction

> Connie and Parkin went slowly down the tussocky hill, above the grey-green country. Across was Haggs Farm. Beyond, Underwood, the mining village and the mines ... And the mill-ponds at Felley lying so still, abandoned, abandoned like everything else that is not coal or iron, away below.[5]

This is virtually the same view that Lawrence describes in his letter to Rolf Gardiner and again points up the contrast of the countryside with the impact of industry that he stresses in his essay on Eastwood and its rural hinterland.

The people

He regularly used the Chambers family as the basis for characters in his early stories as he did many of his friends and Eastwood acquaintances.

Jessie 'the chief friend of my youth' provided the model for Miriam Leivers in *Sons and Lovers;* Emily in *The White Peacock;* Hilda in *Shades of Spring;* and Muriel in *A Modern Lover, The Fly in the Ointment* and several of his poems including *Study, Renascence* and *Last Words to Muriel.* In his first play, *A Collier's Friday Night,* she appears as Maggie Pearson, the surname of the Chambers' neighbours at New Haggs cottage. Alan provides the basis for George Saxton, one of the main characters in *The White Peacock,* plays a leading role in *A Prelude* and also features in *Love among the Haystacks.* Mr and Mrs Chambers appear in *A Prelude, The White Peacock* and *Sons and Lovers;* mainly in straightforward depictions of their life at the farm — domestic duties for Sarah and his farming tasks for Edmund. The two younger boys, Hubert and Bernard, appear in *A Prelude* and *The White Peacock* and provide the basis for Geoffrey and Maurice, the chief male characters in *Love Among the Haystacks,* the short story which draws on Lawrence's time hay-making with the Chambers family in 1908 in the fields near Greasley church. Lawrence uses the same Christian names for the two lads in *Sons and Lovers* where David, the youngest of the family is given his brother Hubert's name. The youngest daughter Molly makes an appearance in *The White Peacock* under her own name but this is the only work in which she appears.

Practical help

Lawrence himself wrote in *Sons and Lovers* that Jessie 'was the threshing floor on which he threshed out all his beliefs' and described her as the 'nurse' of *The White Peacock.* It has been suggested that

> It was not Jessie's criticism he wanted (but) her uncritical encouragement and above all her love for books and literature which made her the right audience ... Jessie was truly a nurse in the sense of one who nurtures and tends.[6]

She was given his poems, multiple drafts of *The White Peacock.* and eventually, and most painfully, *Sons and Lovers* to read and comment upon. But she did more than simply comment. Writing about his early poems in the foreword to *Collected Poems* in 1928, Lawrence said 'I must have burnt many poems ... Save for Miriam, I perhaps should have destroyed them all.' For it was Jessie who, in 1909, sent a selection of his poems to Ford Madox Hueffer, editor of the *The English Review*. The Chambers family had subscribed to the magazine and Jessie recalled 'we were delighted with the journal ... Father thoroughly appreciated it.' Hueffer approved of the poems and published them in November 1909; thus, as Lawrence later wrote, 'the girl had launched me, so easily on my literary career, like a princess cutting a thread, launching a ship.'[7]

Two years earlier, in October 1907, the *Nottinghamshire Guardian* had run a short story competition in three categories:- the most enjoyable Christmas; the best legend of some historic building; and the most amusing Christmas story. Lawrence decided to enter each of the three categories. *A Prelude* was submitted under Jessie's name and proved to be the winning entry in the first category and was published in the newspaper in December 1907 — the first Lawrence work to appear in public, and providing his first earnings from his writing. In the second category he offered, in his own name, *The Legend* (to be published later as *A Fragment of Stained Glass*); he also offered an early version of his story *The White Stocking*, submitted on his behalf by Louie Burrows in the third category. Incidentally, in the same competition, Jessie's younger sister Molly won first prize for the best description of 'how I spent my Christmas holidays.'[8]

Return to the Haggs and its locality

In the preface to this book, John Worthen has discussed the deep sense of nostalgia felt by Lawrence for the Haggs and its family in the moving letter of November 1928 to David Chambers. But this sense of something lost also pervades some of Lawrences early fiction written after he had moved away from Eastwood. In *The White Peacock* Cyril Beardsall, like Lawrence, had left for the south of England where for weeks he was 'haunted by the spirit of some part of Nethermere.' On one of his returns home he finds that 'Nethermere ... had now forgotten me ... I was a stranger, an intruder'[9] even to the birds and flowers by the side of the reservoir. He also discovers that Emily (a new and heavily fictionalised version of the Jessie figure) was soon to marry Tom Renshaw, a farmer from Papplewick, where Emily was now teaching. This same theme appears in two short stories, *A Modern Lover* and *The Shades of Spring,* both written between 1909–12. They share the same story line with the Lawrence figure, Syson in *Shades* and Mersham in *Modern Lover,* who has again left the area, returning to the farm and finding that the Jessie character has found a new lover and that the family were now rather unsympathetic towards him. Both stories contain descriptions of the Haggs Farm and farmhouse, but *Shades of Spring* arguably provides more evidence of Lawrence's empathy with, and consummate ability to describe, the natural world surrounding the farm, and is imbued with the nostalgia that he felt for the place and the people he had known there.

> He loved the place extraordinarily, the hills ranging round. and small red farms like brooches ... to his last day, he would dream of this place, when he felt the sun on his face, or saw the small handfuls of snow between the winter twigs, or smelt the coming of spring.[10]

The best evidence we have for a real-life later return to the vicinity of the Haggs by Lawrence comes in a letter from Willie Hopkin to Harry T. Moore in 1949, describing the author's last visit to Eastwood in September 1926

> 'He and I went over the old ground. When we reached the Felley dam he stood looking over at the Haggs. I sat down by the pool and when I turned to look at him he had a terrible look of pain on his face.'[11]

Conclusion

It is difficult to overstate the important place the Haggs and the Chambers family had in the development of Lawrence as a writer. Much of his early work is based in that rural environment, with the Chambers family members providing models for various characters. The role played by Jessie Chambers in supporting and encouraging Lawrence in his literary ambitions was crucial although it was to cost her dearly during the writing of *Sons and Lovers,* which she regarded as a terrible betrayal of her intimacy with Lawrence and the part she had played in his life.

Haggs Farm stands today, albeit in a decayed condition, as a memorial to the interest in and fascination of the young D.H. Lawrence with the lives of a family and a farming community outside Eastwood; this experience had a massive influence upon his whole development as a writer until, late in life, he began again to write about the area with a nostalgia showing how much it all still meant to him. His feelings had never changed: to call it 'the country of my heart' was an extraordinary tribute to the place — and Haggs Farm was at the centre of it.

Notes

1   *Nottingham and the Mining Countryside, New Adelphi,* 1930
2   *The Prussian Officer* xi 'Lawrence and the Spirit of Place' in *DH Lawrence Miscellany,* 282
    'A Reading of the White Peacock' in *DH Lawrence Miscellany,* 194
3   *The Geographical Background of the Early Works of DH Lawrence* 47 & 57
    The Country of My Heart Nottingham 1972 17 & 22 *DH Lawrence Country* London 1979 44
4   *John Thomas and Lady Jane,* written in 1927
5   *John Worthern: D.H. Lawrence: the Early Years 1885–1912, CUP 1991,* 105
6   *John Worthern: D.H. Lawrence: the Early Years 1885–1912, CUP 1991,* 137
7   'Autobiographical Sketch' – first appeared in the *Sunday Dispatch* on 17th February 1929 as 'Myself Revealed', reprinted in *Phoenix II,* Heinemann 1968
8   Nottinghamshire Archives, Underwood school log books SIL 147/5
9   *The White Peacock* 305–306
10 *The Prussian Officer* 126–127
11 *The Priest of Love* 421

Chapter 4
The Chambers family after the Haggs
Clive Leivers

Arno Vale farm

1910 was an eventful year for the Chambers family. On 10 January Jessie took up a teaching post at Musters Road school in West Bridgford; at the beginning of April the family left the Haggs and moved to Arno Vale Farm or Swinehouse Farm in Arnold; in August the close relationship between Lawrence and Jessie began to break up; and in October Alan married Alvina Reeve, Lawrence's cousin, and left the family home. The move to Arnold may well have been influenced by Jessie taking up her job at West Bridgford and the choice of secondary education available to young David, who was soon to attend Mundella school in Nottingham.

Swinehouse Farm was quite different to the Haggs; it was a larger building of seven rooms; there were some 120 acres attached to the farm as compared to the 35 at the Haggs and the land was of better quality. In a letter to Helen Corke in June 1911 Jessie wrote-

> I can never look at this soil, with its liberal putting forth, without regretting that David knows only the unwilling, stinted growth of the Haggs.[1]

The farm was on the edge of Nottingham's suburbs, with a tram running from the city centre to Mapperley Plains, a short walk from the farm along the footpath to Breckhill Road, a further contrast to the relative isolation of the Haggs. Helen Corke visited the farm on several occasions and described the farmhouse

> hidden in a green hollow approached from the Plains by a steep and irregular footpath winding through hilly pasture. The path ended by the gate of the orchard fronting the house. Stackyard, cowsheds, stable and barns lay beyond[2].

When the family moved from the Haggs, all the children accompanied their parents with the exception of May, who had married Bill Holbrook in 1906; the couple lived in a cottage at Moorgreen until their emigration to Canada. Alan moved out on his marriage and the 1911 census records that he and Alvina — or Tim as she was known to the family — were living nearby at Maitland Road, with Alan's occupation given as a retail milk seller, although he continued to help his father on the farm particularly after his younger brothers Hubert and Bernard emigrated in 1914. Around March 1913 the couple moved to Breckhill Road where they remained for the rest of Alan's life.

So, in 1911 the Arno Vale family consisted of Edmund and Sarah, with five of their children — Jessie (although she had taken lodgings near to her school at West Bridgford), Hubert and Bernard, helping their father with the farm work; Molly, now 15 and helping her mother with the housework; and David aged 12 and still at school. A few years later, in 1914, three of the family had emigrated to Canada — Hubert, Bernard and May, with husband Bill Holbrook. In November 1916 Molly married William Skerritt, a hairdresser from Arnold.

Lawrence and Arno Vale
By the time of the move to Arno Vale in 1910, Lawrence was living and teaching in Croydon and his break with Jessie was imminent. He did however visit the farm on a few occasions and in *A Personal Record* Jessie describes two of the increasingly tense encounters.[3]

When the August holiday came (in 1910) Lawrence suggested that he should spend some days with the family at the new farm, which he had scarcely seen, and we prepared a room for him. He went home first, however, and when I met him several days later, instead of returning with me as he had planned to do, he broke off our engagement completely.

He came to the farm again, a little shy at meeting father ... Mother gave him the same quiet welcome as ever, but father was not the same. The difference was subtle. There was no longer that indefinable attitude of special recognition on father's part. In treating him as some-one quite ordinary he managed to convey a sense of forfeited regard that Lawrence felt acutely ... There was a Sunday when he came to the farm for tea. After tea we stood round the piano singing hymns and folk songs. My younger sister, who was playing the piano, turned to the hymn: "We are but little children weak". I was about to turn the page, saying, we don't want that but Lawrence stopped me impulsively.

'It's true, we are. Let's have it', and he joined in the singing with gusto.

While Lawrence and Jessie continued to meet from time to time, he seemed closer to May Holbrook over the next few years. He visited the Moorgreen cottage and took Frieda and her children there. And his last meeting with Jessie happened there in April 1912. Jessie recalled 'we said goodbye like casual acquaintances ... I never saw him again.'[4]

By March 1913 Jessie had been desperately hurt by the depiction of their relationship in *Sons and Lovers*. She had been destroying his letters and in that month, at May's suggestion, she returned his letter which had accompanied the proofs of the novel — it was their last contact. Apart from a letter to May Holbrook shortly before she emigrated there was no further direct contact between the family and Lawrence until 1928 when Sarah, hearing that Lawrence was unwell, asked her son David to write to him; in response Lawrence wrote his famous letter, full of nostalgia about the Haggs — this was not shown to Jessie until after Lawrence's death in 1930.

Lawrence used the setting of the Arno Vale Farm in *Sons and Lovers*. The location of the farm is accurately portrayed in the description of Morel's meeting and fight with Baxter Dawes:-

One night he left her (Clara) to go to Daybrook station, over the fields ... The town ceases almost abruptly on the edge of a steep hollow. There the houses with their yellow lights stand up against the darkness. He went over the stile and dropped quickly into the hollow of the fields. Under the orchard, one warm window shone in Swineshead Farm ... Some creature stirred under the willows of the farm pond.[5]

By the end of 1913 Jessie had met her future husband — Jack Wood, a fellow teacher, also from a farming background. May was then teaching at the same school as Jack and made the introduction. They married in June 1915 when Jack was in the army; on his discharge, Jessie resigned her teaching post and the couple set up home near her parents on Breckhill Road, where they lived until Jessie's death in 1944.

After Lawrence's death she began a correspondence with Emile Delaveney, who was writing his biography of the writer. The two families met and Jessie took Emile to visit Haggs Farm. He encouraged her to write her own account of the relationship with Lawrence, as did her brother David. *A Personal Record* was published in 1935 and a year later she started to correspond with Koteliansky, who had written to express his appreciation of her memoir. In her reply she described the feeling of liberation that the writing of the book had produced — 'somehow the pain has all evaporated and only joy is left.'[6]

She was certainly able to discuss Lawrence and his critics and biographers quite readily with Kot, as she came to call him, but in a few years began to suffer health problems. In April 1939 she had a stroke and when she and Helen Corke met for the last time a year later, Helen described 'a bent, heavy figure' whom she only recognised with difficulty. After her death in 1944, her husband destroyed all her unpublished work, in accordance with her wishes.

Jessie and Jack on their wedding day

After his days at Mundella school David Chambers graduated at Nottingham University college in 1919 and took up a post as a history teacher at Ashby de la Zouch grammar school in Leicestershire. He then became an adult education lecturer in his home county, married in 1926 and settled with his wife Dorothy on Breckhill Road near his parents, Jessie and Alan. He obtained his PhD in 1927 and after a further spell at Ashby from 1940 to 1946 as head of the history department, he finally became a lecturer, and later professor, at Nottingham University, coming to be regarded as one of the most eminent and respected social and economic historians in the country.

David provided his own account of Lawrence's relationship with the Chambers family in lectures to university students in this country and the USA (see Chapter 2) and in a contribution to the 'Chambers Papers' in Edward Nehl's composite biography which also included May's recollections which had been left with her brother Bernard and which were discovered by David on one of his visits to his brothers in Canada. He also provided an introduction to the second edition of Jessie's *A Personal Record* published in 1965.

So, by 1919 Edmund and Sarah were living alone on the farm, although Alan and Jessie lived close by. Around 1933 the farm and the surrounding area was sold for building and the couple moved to a nearby bungalow on Breckhill Road. Sarah only enjoyed the 'mod cons' at her new home for four years, dying in 1937. Edmund lived another nine years and died in 1946.

The Canadian Emigrants

Bernard and Hubert, by now in their mid-twenties, earned only pocket money on the farm and probably saw little future for themselves in England. In 1913 they left home to work in collieries near Doncaster to raise the boat fare for their move to Canada. They sailed from Liverpool to Halifax, Nova Scotia in March 1914 accompanied by Bill Holbrook. Bill and May had also been considering emigration for some time; Bill was unwell as a result of his stonemason's job and May seems to have had a series of unfulfilling teaching posts; a letter from Lawrence in 1913 mentions Australia as possible destination.

Towards the end of his life Bernard wrote accounts of their early days in Canada and a brief outline is given here. The three men travelled across Canada by train to Saskatchewan and initially took various temporary farm work and other labouring jobs. Bernard and Hubert then took on a homestead some 28

The photograph shows the trio on arrival, with Bill standing behind the two brothers, with Bernard on the left and Hubert to his right.

miles from Turtleford, and seven miles from the nearest store with the nearest neighbour three miles away. To obtain title to the land, they had to break 30 acres of land, build a house and live there for part of each year for three years. They found it bitterly cold; milk would be frozen solid overnight and on one occasion Hubert returned after a day of fruitless hunting for meat unable to speak since his mouth was frozen shut. They continued odd-jobbing until January 1917 when they enlisted in the Canadian Army and went to fight in France. On their return to Canada in the summer of 1919. Hubert returned to the homestead but Bernard received loans from the Soldier Settlement Board and his brother to buy a farmstead near Mervin.

Having found a home Bernard decided he needed to marry and in 1920 wrote to his mother asking for a wife! Lizzie Marsh from Nottingham, a family friend who knew little of her prospective husband, travelled to Canada in February 1921 and the couple married the day after her arrival. The marriage was a success and the couple had three sons — Edmund, Bernard and David — with the result that there are now more descendants of Edmund and Sarah in Canada than in this country.

May Holbrook soon followed her husband, arriving in New York in December 1914, and travelling on to Illinois to live with some of Bill's relatives until she obtained a US teaching certificate in April 1915. Joining Bill in Canada she then had further teacher training in Regina, the capital of Saskatchewan. Her first teaching post was at a settlement of Russian immigrants which must have been quite a challenge. This was followed by posts in a number of schools around Saskatoon. She and Bill settled at Cuffley on Brightsand Lake — about 10 miles from Bernard at Mervin. Their homestead was completed by 1919 when May obtained a local teaching post. She indulged her passion for gardening with her flower garden the talk of the countryside; later she wrote gardening articles under the pen-name of Beet Greens for the local newspaper. She also produced a number of short stories about life in Canada, ran the local debating society and became the unofficial librarian for the district.

In 1949 the couple moved to a bungalow in Sidney on Vancouver Island, British Columbia which had been left them by a school inspector who had known May. They lived there until May died in 1955.

Hubert moved next door to May and Bill in the early 1920s. He never married and died in 1972, spending his final years living with his nephew Edmund.

After what seemed to have been an unsuccessful marriage in 1916, Molly also emigrated in April 1938 with her two sons. She spent some time in Saskatchewan and then moved to British Columbia but had little or no contact with May. She reportedly ran a Xmas tree business and remarried in 1945.

For the Chambers family the 12 years at the Haggs was a relatively short period in their lifetimes. However, for some of the family, the relationship with Lawrence meant life was, in David Chambers words, 'raised to a higher power both in its lights and shades. To know him, as we knew him, was a rare privilege, but it had to be paid for.' This of course applied particularly to Jessie, but the rest of the family were all affected, in varying degrees, by their time at the Haggs. But as this account of their subsequent lives suggests, they discovered new opportunities, new friendships and made the most of them.

Notes

1 *Collected Letters* 13
2 *In Our Infancy* 193
3 ET 182, 1993
4 ET 215
5 *Sons and Lovers* 409
6 *Collected Letters* 134

Chapter 5
Taking root in Canada
May Chambers Holbrook

When David Chambers visited his brother Bernard in Canada in 1956 he found a box of manuscripts written by his sister May 'in the solitude of her prairie schoolhouse.'

They included her recollections of the early life of Lawrence which appear in volume 3 of Edward Nehls' *Composite Biography* and a number of short stories which are now held by the University of Nottingham.

The one chosen here (LaH 76) perhaps best reflects the difficulties faced by May and other immigrant women in settling into their new life.

It is published with the permission of the University and Mrs Ann Howard.

***

May in Canada 1931

Three days alone in the isolated log cabin had reduced Rose Morley to frenzy. She passed out into the white silence and hurried down the trail. The boys had said they would be home last night, and the long empty hours of waiting and listening, through the soundless gloom, and the slow coming daylight, had tortured her. What should she do if anything happened to the boys in this wilderness where help was so far away? The terrible question repeated itself until she felt her helplessness would drive her mad. She found herself running down the trail and checked herself, feeling that she ought to have more control; but soon she was running again, and she didn't care. It was the loose snow that slowed her and presently stopped her. She was panting, but as she rested she grew cold. There was no sound of anyone coming down the trail hidden among the poplars, so close that a deer could not pass between. No sound, no movement, not a bird, not any living thing; and the white mist pressed about her as if it would envelop and absorb her until she was nothing but a wraith. Defeat and fear and defiance mingled in the scream that escaped from her as she turned to retrace her steps.

An hour after she reached the shack, the boys drove in with their loads of lumber, sawn at the distant mill. They had had to wait their turn at the saw, otherwise a pretty good trip they cheerily replied in answer to her anxious questions, and fell ravenously on the hot food she had ready on their plates. Then, pipes going, they sat enjoying the luxury of being home again, and fell asleep.

They argued for days, the men contending that she would get used to it, as they had. 'Anyway' declared her brother, 'you go get us a good permanent job and we'll leave all this; either do that or shut up.'

'Well Rose, if there is anything to go to, I'd leave, but you know how things are. Still I shan't beg you to stay; it's no life for a woman, I know' admitted her husband sorrowfully. 'As you say, I ought never to have let you come; but you wanted to come, and God knows I wanted you. But even though you've lost your job, your folks'll welcome you home again, so you're all right.'

'Well I think you're a quitter' announced her brother, when told she would go out the first time the weather permitted. 'I thought you'd better stuff in you; a woman has a right to stay with her husband. Anyway, what will you do when you get home? — neither married nor single. Just a piker out for the best. Let George do it! That's your motto, eh.'

But the weather was slow to moderate, and in the meantime a young man, looking for a homestead, stayed the night and they talked for hours, delighted to have news that was not a fortnight old like all their letters and newspapers. As he was preparing to go the next day he said shyly 'Say, why don't you come back with me to see my mother, she'd be tickled to death.' After some demur it was arranged she should go, but the young man refused to take her trunk as her brother suggested. 'She'll soon be homesick and glad to come back. Now bundle up good and don't bother to talk. I don't like talking when I'm driving, there's too much to notice.' So, swathed about like a mummy, she made the thirty-five mile trip, and Mrs Goodwin welcomed her after a low word from her son.

Mrs Goodwin had a stunning crown of silver hair and a sensitive face that had a sort of glory to it. Rose could see sweetness and patience and a hint of laughter in it, and some other quality that life had put there for which she could find no name. She's just lovely she told herself and revelled in the snug comfort of the little house.

'It's funny' she said, coming in from exploring her surroundings the first mild day, 'but I've just discovered what I missed most of all on the homestead — the sparrows. Here you have them twittering just as at home, and what an amazing difference they make! The silence made me feel afraid of the unseen; it was uncanny, it lay on you and pressed you down like a terrible threat. Oh. I can never go back to that awful stillness.'

'It is lonely for you' Mrs Goodwin sympathised. 'It's unbearable' said Rose with a shudder. 'Your snug home with its papered walls and covered floors, and all the conveniences of sufficient pots and pans; the telephone and good road with people passing made me feel as if I had come back to life from death, but the twitter of the birds makes it seem like coming back home from death. You have no idea of the horrible effect that deathly stillness can have on a woman. You'd die, I'm sure, up there.'

'I thought so once, but I proved too tough' said Mrs Goodwin merrily. 'But think, we are fifty miles from town' cried Rose. 'Yes, we were further. We went by oxen, did you?' 'No, we have horses, but then I've been used to the car and street-cars' said Rose. 'Ninety miles by oxen, and we came from London' laughed Mrs Goodwin, 'Oh, we were a pair of duffers. It seemed like a picnic, the sunshine, the freedom and space, the wild flowers and fruits. Birds to shoot and fish to catch and a camp fire to cook them by, and the taste! Nothing ever has or ever will taste like those meals by the trail. And the little boys grew fat and brown and jolly. It seemed a different world from the one we had always known, and when we got as far into the wilderness as here, we stopped.' 'Here!' echoed Rose, 'was this ever a wilderness?' 'Twenty-five years ago it was worse than your homestead can be, for fires have gone through year after year and cleaned off the big timber. Then there was shelter for bear as well as deer and moose, and we feasted and fasted, and froze and melted by turns, and we were always happy with the big adventure of it, and healthy with the freedom and the coarse food.'

'Why' exclaimed the girl, 'I can hardly believe it, there's a sweetness about you that gives the impression you had been sheltered from all hardship.' 'I sometimes wonder if hardship is a frame of mind' said Mrs Goodwin thoughtfully. 'It was all very rough and primitive but leading, we believed, to permanent prosperity. It seemed wonderful that vegetables would grow when planted by a complete ignoramus like me, and that a cow would patiently let us get her milk in our clumsy way, and the hens laid, the oats thrived, there was hay for the getting'. 'We've got the key to life' Ted used to say. It seemed like that for three years, and then he was killed helping a neighbour with his well.'

'Oh!' groaned the girl, 'and you with two small children; what did you do?'

'Everything, almost; keeping house, nursing, dressmaking. The neighbour rented my land for the taxes, and I worked till the boys were big enough to take it over. I always had them with me, going to school.' 'You reared two boys and accomplished this?' the girl asked incredulously.

'Don't you think it was the boys who really did it? I had to look out for them; alone, I should naturally have given it up. Their needs drove me to try my strength with the world, and I found such good people, live and let live people, with warm hearts full of kindness to an unfortunate one. I never should have known the real humanity of people if my two little boys had not needed my support. Then when Teddy was sixteen and Len fourteen, we came back here. They looked upon it as a trust from their father. 'I wonder where Dad would have set this building?' 'Do you think we should try wheat on that north aspect?' Always they wondered what dad would have done. 'Wish he could see it now' Teddy would say at harvest. 'You don't know that he can't' Len would declare. And so we fasted oftener than we feasted. Many times, and suffered cold and heat, fought mosquitoes and flies, had losses in crop and stock just like all who love the land and sometimes it seemed very hard, but only to make us try harder, for we loved the life. Every foot of land wrested from the forest, every rock pile and every fence, has its own personal association. The homestead becomes part of its people, they toil and sweat over it to bring it to cultivation, they plan and scheme and deny themselves for it, till at last it repays them with a living, scant maybe at times, but there is nothing quite so satisfying as your own land. It is a world of your own, a kingdom won by determination and toil and love of achievement, and it teems with interest because it has to do with life itself.

She stopped abruptly, then asked comically 'Don't you think I'd qualify for a soap-box orator in Hyde Park? Like a dear old friend of mine would say, I get "all het up" talking about the farm.'

After a pause the girl said in a low voice 'Now I know the quality in your face that eluded me; it's bravery or steadfastness, and you've made me feel a puny whining cry-baby. But tell me one thing, when do the sparrows come?' 'Just as soon as a little grain got scattered about, and a few sheaves stacked. Besides, you'll have a windbreak some day, then all the birds of the forest are at your door.' 'Is it too late for Len to start home with me today?' 'Of course it is.' 'Well then, tomorrow?'

'We'll see' smiled Mrs Goodwin. But it was a week before she deemed the time ripe for Rose to go home, and stay home; and by that time Rose was ready to walk, if they didn't soon take her. 'For' she explained 'what you did for the memory of your husband, I can at least help mine to do.'

Chapter 6
The friendship of Helen Corke and Jessie Chambers
Clive Leivers

Introduction

Jessie and Helen first met in 1910 and for the next two years had a close friendship. This period covered the time when Lawrence was asking Jessie for comments on the drafts of *Sons and Lovers* and which she described as 'the most difficult bit of my life.' Helen became her confidante and Jessie paid tribute to her sympathetic response — 'she helped me to gather together some fragments of my shattered self-confidence' after the final break with Lawrence. But looking at that friendship one is always conscious of a presence in the background — that of Lawrence, who was instrumental in bringing the two women together and whose later conduct contributed to the decline in the intensity of that relationship.

Helen Corke, 1903

That first meeting in July 1910 happened during a weekend spent by Jessie in Croydon visiting Lawrence; the three shared a walk on Hayes Common. Helen was immediately attracted to Jessie — or Muriel as she was invariably called by Lawrence and Helen. Jessie was then 24, Helen four years older.

Helen before the first meeting

Helen was born in Hastings in 1882, the eldest child of Alfred and Louisa Corke. Her given Christian name was actually Nellie as evidenced by her birth registration and census returns — and various correspondents including Jessie and Lawrence refer to her as Nell — but perhaps this was a name which did not fit the persona she cultivated with Lawrence and Jessie who always wrote to her as Helen (e) or even Sieglinde — a name taken from Wagner! In return

Helen addressed her letters to Muriel, a name used often by Lawrence when writing about Jessie.

Helen's father originally owned a series of small grocery shops, none of which thrived and by 1891 he had become an insurance agent. On leaving school, she tried various clerical jobs, but then returned to her old school as a pupil teacher. Following the same path as Lawrence and Jessie she attended a Pupil Teachers centre, gained her teacher's certificate and obtained a post in a Croydon school becoming 'a cog in an instruction machine.'[1]

At the age of 19 she started to learn the violin, later taking lessons from the married Herbert MacCartney, a professional musician. She began to feel something of love for him; his feelings moved to the 'physical plane' and in 1909 they went together for a holiday at Freshwater in the Isle of Wight. This failed to resolve the difference in their feelings and after returning home MacCartney committed suicide. The story of their failed romance became the subject of Lawrence's second published novel *The Trespasser.*

Helen had first met Lawrence in the autumn of 1908 at the home of Agnes Mason, a close friend and fellow teacher with Lawrence at the Davidson Road school. Initially the pair met only infrequently but the following year the friendship became a close one with Lawrence visiting the Corke home regularly on three evenings a week. For Helen it was a brother and sister relationship, but Lawrence was sexually attracted to her and ultimately proposed marriage. This Helen rejected, recording that she neither wished to be his wife nor mistress.[2]

Helen & Jessie

After their first meeting the friendship of the two women blossomed with a frequent exchange of letters, visits to each other's home and regular holidays together. Helen wrote that Jessie's letters 'confirmed my ... impression of her rare quality and intuitional power; they also reflected the suffering inflicted ... by the long conflict with Lawrence.'[3]

That meeting in July was quickly followed by Jessie visiting Helen at her parents' home in August, the month in which Lawrence broke off their engagement. During this trip Helen showed her the places associated with the happiest part of her childhood, in particular Newhaven on the south coast where her grandparents had lived. They shared memories — Jessie of the

Haggs and her relationship with Lawrence; Helen of her childhood by the sea and her association with MacCartney.

Jessie wrote in that month 'I owe you a great debt for the privilege of being able to talk to you'; this was especially valuable as she was unable to confide in her family about the deteriorating relationship with Lawrence and had no other close friend in Nottinghamshire.[4]

In the October of 1910 Helen paid her first visit to the Chambers family at Arno Vale. They went for long walks in the countryside of Jessie's childhood and adolescence with the result that for Helen *'The White Peacock* becomes life rather than literature.'[5] This first visit was followed by a week at the farm during the Xmas holidays. Between those visits Jessie's relationship with Lawrence underwent a further blow with his engagement to Louie Burrows and prior to the visit she wrote to Helen saying 'I think I must not talk about him at all. At present I am not strong enough.'[6]

Helen recalled the visit showed that the pair 'were so much attuned that we could talk frankly of intimate matters, read one another's written work, or just remain silent.'[7] Jessie's letters show how her friendship with Helen took the place of her former intimacy with Lawrence. They exchanged books, commenting on their shared reading — authors such as Verlaine, Turgenev, Meredith and George Moore. Jessie sent Helen drafts of her own writing for comment — particularly the novel *The Rathe Primrose* which Helen encouraged her to send to Edward Garnett for comment. The holiday ended with three days walking in Derbyshire, having first stayed overnight with the Holbrooks in Moorgreen. New Year's Eve 1910 saw them walking from Matlock Bath into Matlock along the riverside. They then took the funicular railway from the centre of Matlock up to Smedley's Hydro.

When Jessie stayed at Croydon she was always keen to see the neighbouring countryside since the south of England was terrain as fresh to her as the Midlands were to Helen. There were trips into London, visiting art galleries, attending classical concerts and viewing the sights from open-top buses.

At Whitsun in 1911 Helen again visited Arno Vale, travelling by a night excursion train and arriving in Nottingham at 5am where she was met by Jessie who took her to Mapperley on the first tram of the day. During this stay the women took the train to Mablethorpe, where Jessie had previously spent a holiday with the Lawrence family.

During the summer holidays of 1911 Helen planned to take Jessie to see her brother Arthur at Plymouth; they were unable to take the expected boat journey because of a dock strike, travelled instead by train only to find that a railway strike was planned for the next day so returned to Croydon the day after their arrival. Helen wrote 'this is my introduction to the revolt of labour (whereas) the struggle between Capital and Labour is a cogent reality' to Jessie who subsequently introduced her to active members of the local Labour and Independent Labour Parties.[8]

In a letter of September that year Jessie asked how Helen was affected by the 'swift transition from one individuality to another' — herself and Lawrence. Helen wrote 'with Muriel I have always a sense of encompassing warmth ... I rest content in the present moment ... with David I never rest ... we are always wandering ... in a spiritual wilderness.'[9]

Despite the growing breach in their relationship Jessie remained in touch with Lawrence, asking him to take some apples from the Arno Vale orchard to Helen and baking him a birthday cake. In the November of that year Lawrence developed pneumonia and that illness ended his time in Croydon and his teaching career. After convalescing in Bournemouth, he returned to Eastwood. Helen met him briefly in February 1912 but never saw him again after that. Helen recognised that 'my life ... moves on towards its next stage. For two years it has been polarised between David & Muriel. Now the stresses change.'[10]

Lawrence continued work on *Sons and Lovers* sending drafts to Jessie for comment. She came to view the depiction of the relationship between Paul and Miriam as, in Helen's words, 'a terrible distortion of the truth — by this betrayal of her faith in him, he had defaced his own image ... Jessie had to work out, alone, a reorientation of her spirit ... A vital section of her world had been torn away.' Jessie saw the book as giving 'the death blow to our friendship ... in the passing of Lawrence I saw the extinction of my greater self; life without him was a bleak aspect.'[11]

Helen saw this reflected in Jessie's letters from which 'the spontaneity and lyricism disappeared.' During the summer of 1912 she detected the impact on Jessie's personality — 'the lamp of her spirit burned low ... her fine poise, her quiet self-confidence left her; she moved as if in an enemy world, warily. The consciousness of an intimate understanding between us blurred.'[12]

They went for a holiday in the Rhineland in August. Helen recalled 'It was an empty experience ... Jessie sat absorbed in *The Brothers Karamazov* ... all the time I felt, curiously, that I was alone.' She added 'the warm, vivid Muriel of the past two years is changing; her fire is sinking ... at this moment I do not understand how I, to Muriel, have been simply a mirror reflection of the self of David which she loved, and now cannot even pretend exists.'[13]

Helen wrote that, later on, she came to realise that their friendship was inspired by Lawrence; she had served as a link between them during 1911 — but as Jessie rejected him, so she turned from Helen. But Jessie responded in January 1913 'I am not sure whether the changes in me are so great as you think ... I think that in time harmony between us will come of its own accord ... a new kind of sympathy perhaps.'[14]

In the spring of 1913 Jessie returned the final proofs of *Sons and Lovers* unopened and wrote to Helen — 'If he doesn't soon let me alone, he'll be the death of me ... The Miriam part of the novel is a slander — a fearful treachery ... Don't talk about it please. If I am to live at all it will be necessary to put David out of my life ... Please, please digest this quickly & get it over before I come.'[15]

In 1913 Helen was hoping that Jessie might come to Croydon to teach but in May Jessie felt she could never live there. But after a visit by Helen that month when a planned excursion to Lincoln was abandoned in favour of a weekend spent with May Holbrook, Jessie wrote to her sister enthusing about the friendship.

> 'I think I shall look upon this weekend as unique; there seemed to be perfect harmony, a rare state ... I shall look back (on it) with gladness and confidence — like to a beauty spot on a rather uphill road.'

In August that year Jessie visited the family of Marc Boutrit, her French penfriend; she wrote to Helen 'I am very happy here. The life is ... not so much different from, say, life at the Haggs' and in Helen's view Jessie returned 'soothed & strengthened ... with a quiet spirit'.[16]

After this, the next surviving letter from Jessie is in August 1914 in which she expresses her horror about the imminent war. By this time of course she had met Jack Wood whom she was to marry in June 1915. In March, Helen had written that she could no longer picture Jessie in any known surroundings or society; Jessie replied that 'I'm afraid it is doomed to be so, for the present at any rate' adding that 'a sane & healthy man's attitude is a fine tonic.'[17] The two women seldom met after Jessie's marriage and the occasional visits became increasingly disappointing, Helen feeling that Jessie had 'retreated into domesticity.'

Then the news of Lawrence's death in 1930 brought further correspondence. Jessie wrote asking if Helen had maintained contact with him or had any news to pass on. (She hadn't.) And later wrote again acknowledging that knowing Lawrence 'has helped me to extend enormously the territory of life and that is a godlike thing to do.'[18]

In 1933 Helen sent a copy of her essay on Lawrence's *Apocalypse*. Jessie replied 'I can't wax enthusiastically about it, because it is concerned with that aspect of DHL that I have always found least interesting. As an artist, when he is dealing with the immediate & the concrete, he is superb, but when he essays to be a thinker, I find him superficial & unconvincing & soon quite boring.'[19] This was the last letter from Jessie to survive and was signed Jessie Wood, rather than Muriel — to Helen this was a further indication of the widened distance between their perceptions of Lawrence and his work; but perhaps for Jessie simply a plain statement that she was no longer the Muriel that Helen had known.

They met for the last time in 1940 in a Nottingham café. Helen described a 'bent, heavy figure' whom she only recognised with difficulty. She found conversation virtually impossible with Jessies's deafness and the noise of the café. The only emotion she felt was pity and was unable to make any real contact.[20]

Four years later Jessie died, but in 1951 Helen resumed contact with the Chambers family. That year saw the publication of her memoir of Jessie, *DH Lawrence's Princess,* and she wrote to David Chambers expressing relief that he approved of the book. In the summer of 1972 she visited the *Young Bert* exhibition in Nottingham and stayed with David's daughter Ann and her husband Geoff Howard. She was then in her ninetieth year but Ann recalled that she was a petite, amazingly energetic woman, who was totally fascinated by all the exhibits. She died in 1978 at the age of 96.

Notes

1 Helen Corke, *In Our Infancy*, 1975
2 Ibid 191
3 Helen Corke, *DH Lawrence's 'Princess'*, 1951
4 *Collected Letters* 8
5 *In Our Infancy* 194
6 *Collected Letters* 14
7 *Princess* 20
8 *In Our Infancy* 205–56
9 Ibid 207
10 Ibid 218
11 *Princess* 30–31
12 *Princess* 31–32
13 *In Our Infancy* 220
14 *Collected Letters* 25
15 Ibid 27
16 Ibid 41
17 Ibid 45
18 Ibid 51
19 Ibid 53
20 *Princess* 48

Chapter 7
Conversations

The first two pieces in this chapter are transcripts of interviews between David Chambers and Tony Church, around 1964–66, discussing the possibility of preserving Haggs Farm; and secondly talking to Bridget Pugh about Lawrence's depiction of the Haggs in his fiction.

The third item records a conversation between the late George Hardy, who was a leading light in the Eastwood Historical Society and Charlotte Stevens (née Rockley), then in her nineties, who had lived at the neighbouring Felley Farm between 1885 and 1897.

David Chambers (JDC) talking to Tony Church (TC)

TC   Professor David Chambers speaking about the move that's being made to preserve Haggs Farm

JDC I think it's a very good idea. First of all I think we ought to do something like this. If we don't do something of this kind it would really become something of a reflection on the county itself. What would we feel if it allowed all associations with Byron to fall into decay? Lawrence is one of the great world figures, he's certainly the greatest literary figure that Nottinghamshire has ever produced, and I feel we owe it to ourselves and to the reputation of the county throughout the world, that we should do something about it, and if we could do it in that form that seems to me probably the best way that we could recognise our obligation to Lawrence and his relationship with us as members of this county.

TC   We tried to get in touch with the present owner, Sir William Barber, to see what he felt about it. We rang him up. We couldn't get him, he seemed to be unavailable. We did get Lady Barber and she made it very clear that she and Sir William see no reason for preserving the Haggs, as she put it 'as a shrine to D.H. Lawrence.' And that anyway they don't like Lawrence and people in the district didn't like Lawrence. Now would this be at all because Lawrence tended to use people that he knew and were close to him?

JDC Well, I think it would. A number of people feel that he did undoubtedly take local characters and present them in ways which were easily recognisable by people who knew them and then put them in situations which were quite foreign to their nature, and to that extent Lawrence has opened himself to very serious criticism, and indeed no-one would be more willing to criticise him on those grounds than I would myself, but I don't think that this is a reason for trying to disassociate ourselves with the Lawrence connection. Lawrence is unquestionably a great figure and it's rather petty, it seems to me, on our part to remember that aspect of his work; after all, he was a great artist and a great artist has to use his material in the way that he thinks best. As for Sir William's relationship to this, I would think that it is not a very serious one. I'm not in a position to say to what extent Lawrence used Sir William in his work, but even if he did, and I'm quite sure it was not on an important scale, then I shouldn't have thought that that was a good reason for refusing to have anything to do with attempts to keep our memory of Lawrence fresh, and that is all we are trying to do, especially for the benefit of people in other parts of the world who may have no interest whatever in this purely local connection with Lawrence.

TC You and your family lived at the Haggs and you're in some way involved personally with the Haggs. How much are you involved in this particular issue personally?

JDC I certainly did live at the Haggs. I was born there, I knew Lawrence there very well. I remember those days very vividly, but I do feel that it should be made quite clear that our object and my object is to make the Haggs available to people who want to understand Lawrence and are genuinely interested in him. As for my personal association with it, that's of no consequence whatsoever.

TC If it were turned into a museum, what would you like to see there that would reflect life as it was when you knew the Haggs, and in some way really reflect Lawrence?

JDC I would make it look bright and cheerful, because if there's one thing about our association with Lawrence, it was that it was such a happy one. As far as I was concerned, extremely happy. We had a very gay time with him at the Haggs and I would like to reproduce that gaiety if I could. As for what would go inside is rather more difficult. I think it would be quite possible to get the kind of furniture we had — the old piano, a very old piano which nearly always went wrong because we battered it so — we had to patch it up every time we had one of our parties, and of course Lawrence was the key figure in those parties; and I would like to see old-fashioned furniture and a big oval table in the parlour as we called it; and if we had it fixed up in that way I think it would reproduce that atmosphere of Lawrence — that's the only kind of way that I can think of doing it.

Locations in *The White Peacock*

Bridget Pugh (BP) was a tutor in the Adult Education Department at Nottingham University and this conversation between her and David Chambers about the accuracy of Lawrence's depiction of the Haggs farmhouse in *The White Peacock* and *Sons and Lovers* was originally broadcast on Radio Nottingham. She later produced a well-known booklet on *The Country of My Heart* for the Nottinghamshire Local History Council in 1972 which was initially sold in aid of the David Chambers Memorial Fund, which would help to establish the framework-knitting museum at Ruddington.

BP The description in *The White Peacock* of the farm kitchen (Chapter 1) reads:-

   'George, indifferent to all claims, continued to read. It was very annoying to watch him pulling his brown moustache and reading indolently while the dog rubbed against his leggings and against the knee of his old riding breeches. He would not even be at the trouble to play with Trip's ears.'

   Now you said Trip was a real dog.

JDC Oh yes. That was his name. Oh, very much a real dog. Splendid bull terrier. White all over.

BP   He then goes on to describe the room:- 'The little square window above him filtered a green light from the foliage of the great horse chestnut outside.'

JDC Yes, well, that's perfectly true except that I don't think it was a horse chestnut. My memory is that it consisted of — the foliage was — of two cherry trees. We had two magnificent cherry trees there, and they were very good bearers of cherries. We got large quantities from them.

BP   It's very interesting that he uses that elsewhere where he pelts one of your sisters with cherries.

JDC Yes, I'm quite willing that would have happened too. He often got up into that cherry tree. My father climbed up it and made it bend over, bringing the cherries down with him.

BP   Then he goes on — 'The kitchen was very big.'

JDC No, that I think is where he is mixing up the kitchen with what we called the parlour. The parlour was a big room, and that is where we had these magnificent charades and a big parlour table on which he sat and drove the coach horses. I remember very well. The kitchen was a very tiny room really with a staircase taken out of it. It was a very irregular room and there was a corner window under which he may very well have sat. The description of my brother reading and taking no notice of his dog or anything else is absolutely true. That is perfectly as it would happen — over and over again — and casually curling his brown moustache. Yes, yes, that's absolutely true.

BP   And to go on then. This is still the parlour is it? — 'The table looked lonely, and the chairs mourned darkly for the lost companionship of the sofa.'

JDC Yes

BP   Now what about this? — 'The chimney was a black cavern away at the back.'

JDC Oh yes, that's true. That's the chimney of the kitchen. It's the same place as he's referring to my mother cooking potatoes and so on, isn't it?

BP   Yes, that's it.

JDC Yes well you see she did. There was an old-fashioned grate there with a hob on either side and a boiler — the only source of hot water apart from the kettle we had at that time. It was of course a coal fire and I suppose could be described as a black cavern. That makes it sound rather big. I shouldn't have thought that it was as big as would quite justify that description — but still, there was a fire there, the hob on one side, the oven on the other and that is the only method we had of cooking and getting hot water.

BP   He's amalgamated two rooms I should think.

JDC Yes, he's amalgamated two rooms.

BP   To go on. Is this parlour or kitchen? — 'The only gay things were the chintz coverings of the sofa and the armchair cushions, bright red in the bare sombre room.'

JDC Well that would be true of the parlour. It wouldn't be true of the kitchen because we hadn't room for all that. We had a very short sofa just long enough for one side of the table and enough chairs to enable six or seven of us to sit down. There was nothing in the way of chintz coverings and that sort of thing.

BP   And not even the old clock?

JDC Oh, the clock was there. Oh yes.

BP   That was in the kitchen?

JDC I've got it now. I've still got the old clock.

BP   Well then — the other description of the kitchen. This is what he says in *Sons and Lovers* (Chapter 7). He says that it was 'small and irregular.'

JDC That's right, that's the kitchen.

BP   'The farm had originally been a labourer's cottage. And the furniture was old and battered. But Paul loved it, loved the sack bag that formed the hearthrug, and the funny little corner under the stairs, and the small window deep in the corner through which, bending a little, he could see the plum trees in the back garden and the lovely round hills beyond.'

JDC   He got the kitchen there perfectly.

Recollections of the Barber family and life at Felley

Charlotte Rockley was born at Felley Farm in 1885 and lived there until the age of 12. Her family were close neighbours of the Leivers at the Haggs and her father worked for the Barber family of Lamb Close. The following extracts from her interview with George Hardy provide valuable first-hand memories of life in the Felley Valley and schooldays at Underwood.

Life at Felley

GH   Did you like it down at Felley?

CR   Yes, we didn't feel a bit lonely. There was a lot of people in summertime. Before they fenced the reservoir off you could sit on the grass at the side of the water. Brake-loads of people used to come from Nottingham, used to put their horses up at the Horse and Groom (a public house at Moorgreen) and walk down to the reservoir, have a picnic down there ... it used to be a nice holiday for them. It wasn't lonely, not down there.

GH   I don't think the Chambers family would have moved into Haggs Farm before you left?

CR   No, I don't think they had. Leiverses lived there a long long time. The old lady, we used to call her Granny Leivers. (This was Selina, the grandmother of Charlotte's contemporaries living at the Haggs.) She was ever so good; if mother wasn't very well or something like that, she'd soon be across.

GH   Was she the one who fetched the flour?

CR   Yes, she put it on her head — she didn't hold it, she had her hands on her hips and used to carry it. Same with her groceries — she had a big basket of groceries — used to have that on her head with her hands on her hips.

GH   Who was your schoolmaster at Underwood?

CR   Mr Stringfellow, he lived at School House. We all used to meet at the
     top of the road where you go down to Haggs Farm. There used to be
     Alice Leivers and Lizzie Leivers — they lived at Haggs Farm then.
         And there was a lot of us and we used to have to take a bit of lunch.
     There was no hot dinners and that then. And then at dinner time —
     there was no water laid at Underwood; there was a road facing the school
     and you went down it and there was a pump. You got to go there for
     your water. And us girls what had gone from Felley, Mrs Stringfellow
     used to say sometimes — 'shall you go and fetch me a bucket of water
     from the pump?'

The Barber family

GH   Did you know the family well?

CR   Oh yes, there was a little group of their people and their families. At
     Christmas, there was always a party for the workers' children. There was
     a party and a Christmas tree and a gift for each child — an apple and an
     orange. You used to take your own bags for sweets and there was always
     something to wear; sometimes you'd get a coat or material to make a
     dress — something like that, always something useful. (Mabel Thurlby,
     one of Lawrence's childhood friends recalled that the children were given
     an orange and a 'bright new penny.' Lawrence was too shy to collect his
     presents from the butler, so Mabel collected the gifts on his behalf.) Then
     we would play games — all round the house (Lamb Close) just one room
     that was sealed; I think it was Mr Barber's room that you weren't
     allowed in. Used to go all over and Barber's children used to play with
     us. There was Norman Barber — he was the youngest.

GH   You knew Cissie then? (Cissie Barber was drowned in Moorgreen
     reservoir aged six; the tragedy was used by Lawrence in *Women in Love*.)

CR   Oh yes, she used to play with us when we used to go. And then, later
     on, there was a ball for the mothers and fathers. My mother and dad
     used to go. They used to bring us children home in the heavy cart —

we didn't like riding. We had a toy each when we went to this Christmas treat.

GH   Was that every year then?

CR   Yes.

GH   And did it carry on after Thomas died? (Thomas Barber died aged 50 in 1893.)

CR   Oh yes. Children had theirs at Christmas. The parents had theirs in the New Year. Oh, they was ever so good people. Mr Barber he was so generous during the strike; they had the old slaughterhouse at Oaks Farm, they used to kill so many sheep a week and make soup for the miners when they were out on strike.

GH   What was this about his giving them (the workmen) so much money?

CR   As many years as they had been there, they got as many pounds.

GH   When did he give them this?

CR   When Mr Barber died, it was in his will that you got a pound for every year. My dad had been there 20 years, so he got £20. He had a melodeon with some of this money — it had got pearl keys.

GH   He had a big staff at Lamb Close in those days didn't he?

CR   Oh yes. There were pantry boys, kitchen maids and cook — chefs and everything. And at each doorway when they propped it open, there was like a doll dressed like a servant. It had got a black dress on, and apron with a bib on and strings at the back and a cap on. It was stood against the door to keep the door open. (The 1891 census records nine female servants living at Lamb Close — a governess, two nurse maids, cook, kitchen maid, two house maids, a laundress and a seamstress.)

GH   What was Mrs Barber like?

CR   A nice person, not very tall, nice looking.

Chapter 8
Letters of Jessie Chambers to Willie Hopkin

The collected letters of Jessie — mainly to Helen Corke, Emile Delavenay and Koteliansky were published in the *D.H. Lawrence Review* in 1979.

Two other letters from Jessie are among some correspondence of Willie Hopkin deposited in Nottinghamshire Archives (DD 670/2/1–2).

Together with Lawrence, Jessie was a regular attender at the Hopkin's house in Eastwood where they discussed social issues, literature and religion.

Jessie shared Hopkin's left-wing sympathies, though playing no active role as Willie did. She knew the leaders of the Independent Labour Party (ILP) in Selston when living at the Haggs and gave a lecture on Keats to a study group in the village — 'one of the most memorable classes' given by 'a brilliant young socialist'.[1]

Writing to Koteliansky a couple of years after the first of the Hopkin letters, Jessie recalled that what turned her into a pacifist was 'the tremendous swindle of all that sacrifice.'[2]

The first letter suggests that this was the first contact for some years and shows Jessie's commitment to pacifism at a time when the threat of war was increasing; the second, sent five years later indicates further contact in the intervening period; Jessie by now knew the name of Hopkin's second wife and she no longer felt the need to add her surname to the good wishes. The letter includes a touching reference to Lawrence, showing that any bitterness Jessie had felt earlier was now overshadowed by more happy memories. Both were sent from her home at Breckhill Road, Woodthorpe. No other letters are in the archive, but contact seems to have continued — Jack Wood wrote to tell Hopkin of Jessie's death the day after the event.

March 18th 1936.

Dear Willie,
What a pity you didn't begin 'Dear Jessie.' Please do in future, I'm no lover of formality for its own sake.

Thank you for forwarding Frieda Lawrence's letter. I am sending a reply to the Hollywood address. If she has moved on, I suppose it will be forwarded.

Jack thanks you for your garnered information; he thinks you are right but hopes you are wrong. However time will show.

I thought the enclosed pamphlet might interest you, if you have not already seen it. It is very interesting to find Aldous Huxley taking up a definite standpoint on such a fundamental issue. It seems to me that Pacifism is the chief thing worth working for just now. Please keep the pamphlet and would you be good enough as to show it to anyone you think might be interested.

We shall be delighted to see you both here very shortly, but don't expect great things of our garden. We have our full share of failures. The joy of gardening is the main thing, but there hasn't been a chance to do any since last October. Things are beginning to look up a bit now, though. We hope you have quite got rid of the phlebitis trouble, and also that Mrs Hopkin is keeping well (there I must perforce adopt the formal address through ignorance).

With kindest regards from both of us.

Yours very sincerely
Jessie Wood

PS I think it was very nice of Mrs Lawrence to tell me that she had enjoyed reading my book.

(Hopkin had received a letter from Frieda Lawrence in February 1936 which began 'I read Miriam's book and I wish you would send her this letter.')

December 2nd 1941

Dear WH,

Thank you very much indeed for the copy of the *Nottingham Journal* with the splendid drawing of you by Stanley Parker, and the delightful article. I shall pass it on to father; he always enjoys reading about you.

I wonder if I might be permitted to share the secret of the original character for the portrayal of Lady Chatterley? Or is she one more of the composite characters DHL was so apt at producing, always with more than a little of himself in the make-up!

If it isn't presumptuous to say so, I should like to take this opportunity of saying that as far as I am concerned, I am entirely at peace concerning DHL. We were both wrong and both right, and the combined circumstances were too much for us. I remember him very tenderly, as who could help, who had known him as completely as I had.

I hope you are both well. We have both got slight colds. Although Christmas is

78

more than three weeks away, I'm going to send my best wishes to you both for a very happy Christmas and prosperous New Year.

With love to Betty

Yours very sincerely
Jessie[3]

Notes

1   David Wheatley, *'Matt' From Mines to Minds*, 40
2   *Collected Letters of Jessie Chambers*
3   *Collected Letters of Jessie Chambers*

Haggs 2022

Postscript

The Haggs looks tired and decayed now; it may even fall down. But it will be seen as long as Lawrence's writings live, with honeysuckle and Virginia creeper round the porch, and a water-pippin at the door and my mother in her apron coming out to meet him.

David Chambers: Introduction to the second edition of *A Personal Record* 1965.

Select Bibliography

Corke H, *D.H. Lawrence's 'Princess'* Merle Press, Thames Ditton, 1951,
   In Our Infancy CUP, Cambridge 1975
ET (Jessie Chambers) *D.H. Lawrence: A Personal Record* (3rd edition) CUP, Cambridge 1980
Gajdusek R. 'A Reading of *The White Peacock*' in *D.H. Lawrence Miscellany*
   Heinemann, London 1967
Lawrence D.H. *The Prussian Officer and Other Stories,* Grafton, London 1994
   'Nottingham and the Mining Countryside' in *Phoenix,* Viking Press, New York 1936
   Sons and Lovers, CUP, Cambridge 1992
   The White Peacock, CUP, Cambridge 1983
   Letters Volumes I and VI CUP, Cambridge 1979 and 1991
Moore H.T. (ed) *D.H. Lawrence Miscellany* Heinemann, London 1967
   The Priest of Love Heinemann, London 1974
Nehls E. *D.H. Lawrence; A Composite Biography* Vol III University of Wisconsin Press,
   Madison 1959
Pugh B *The Country of My Heart* Nottinghamshire Local History Council, Nottingham 1972
Scharer M 'Lawrence and the Spirit of Place' in *D.H. Lawrence Miscellany*
   Heinemann, London 1967
Sinzelle C.M. *The Geographical Background of the Early Works of D.H. Lawrence*
   Didier, Paris 1964
Spencer R. *D.H. Lawrence Country* Cecil Woolf, London 1980
Wheatley D. *'Matt' From Mines to Minds* Milward & Sons, Nottingham 1967
Worthen J. *D.H. Lawrence: The Early Years* 1885–1912, CUP, Cambridge 1991
Zytaruk G.J. (ed) *The Collected Letters of Jessie Chambers D.H. Lawrence Review*
   XII Spring-Summer 1979.